*Edited and translated by*
*Kay Pritchett*

# FOUR POSTMODERN POETS OF SPAIN

*A Critical Introduction with Translations of the Poems*

The University of Arkansas Press

*Fayetteville* ◆ *London* ◆ ◆ *1991*

*Designer:* Chiquita Babb
*Typeface:* Sabon

The paper used in this publication meets the minimum
requirements of the American National Standard for
Permanence of Paper for Printed Library Materials
Z39.48-1984. ∞

Publication of this volume was supported by a grant from
The Program for Cultural Cooperation between Spain's
Ministry of Culture and United States Universities.
We would like to thank the following literary agent and
publishers for permission to reprint formerly published
texts: Agencia Literaria Carmen Balcells, Ediciones
Hiperión, and Visor Libros.

*Library of Congress Cataloging-in-Publication Data*

Four postmodern poets of Spain : a critical introduction
with translations of the poems / edited and translated by
Kay Pritchett with additional translations by John DuVal
and Manuel López.
   p.  cm.
  English and Spanish.
  ISBN 1-55728-173-4 (alk. paper).—ISBN 1-55728-174-2
(pbk. : alk. paper)
   1. Spanish poetry—20th century.  2. Spanish poetry—
20th century—Translations into English.  3. English
poetry—Translations from Spanish.  I. Pritchett, Kay,
1946–  .  II. DuVal, John, 1940–  .  III. López,
Manuel.
PQ6187.F68  1991
861'.6408—dc20                                          90-33978
                                                              CIP

# FOUR
# POSTMODERN
# POETS OF
# SPAIN

*In memory of my parents,*
*E. V. and Elizabeth Pritchett*

# ACKNOWLEDGMENTS

Of the help and encouragement I have received from institutions, colleagues, friends, and family members, I would like to especially thank the Program for Cultural Cooperation between Spain's Ministry of Culture and United States Universities for a subvention grant; the Fulbright Foundation and the University of Arkansas for travel and research funds; Manuel Vázquez Montalbán, Antonio Colinas, Guillermo Carnero, and Pere Gimferrer for permission to translate their poetry; the latter four and José María Castellet for information provided for the introduction; and Larry Stephen Perry, reference librarian at the University of Arkansas, for his help in locating materials.

## *List of Contributors*

John DuVal: "Snares" (Gimferrer); "Avila," "Perpetual Motion," "Les Charmes de la vie," "Setting Sail for Cythera" (Carnero); "Novalis," "La Corona," "The River of Shadow" (Colinas).

Manuel López: "Ode to Venice While Watching the Sea on a Stage," "Band of Angels" (Gimferrer).

All other poems were translated by the editor.

# CONTENTS

# PREFACE

Spain's literary experience throughout the twentieth century has rivaled its political temperament in exuberance, diversity, and conflict. Sometimes literary movements have developed at the center of political strife, polarizing writers engaged in similar artistic endeavors. At other times, as in the Generation of 1898, strife created a commonality of purpose: writers as diverse as Unamuno, Baroja, Azorín, Valle-Inclán, and Machado discovered signs of a national identity in the artifacts of Spain's history and landscape.

In the twenties Spain experienced a major revival in poetry as the young writers of the Generation of 1927—Lorca, Alberti, Aleixandre, Guillén, Salinas, Cernuda, and others—took up the folkloric tradition of Spanish verse, so artfully employed earlier by Antonio Machado and Juan Ramón Jiménez, and blended its forms and resonances with the literary innovations of the European avant-garde. The clash between Nationalists and Republicans in the Civil War of 1936–1939 broke up this literary community: Lorca was assassinated several months before the first battle; and several other writers went into exile, some dying as expatriates, others returning only when democracy was restored in the mid-seventies. An exception, Vicente Aleixandre remained behind to become the mentor of numerous poets of succeeding generations and in 1977 received the Nobel Prize for Literature.

The Civil War, which crushed the century's first attempt at democracy, created in its wake new generations of writers. Men and women who raised their voices above the closely-watched silence of Franco's regime formed three generations of postwar poets. The first and second generations experienced the war as children or young adults, but the third, born after the war, also called *novísimos* ("very recent ones"), experienced only its aftermath of poverty, disease, repression, and censorship.

Much poetry of the forties and early fifties, generally called "social" poetry, reflected these harsh conditions, whose influence gradually faded over time. Nevertheless, many critics of the sixties and seventies persisted in evaluating postwar poetry against the canons of the earlier style, limiting and possibly undermining their readings of these texts. Then, in 1982, Andrew P. Debicki's careful analysis of texts from the second postwar generation (Brines, Rodríguez, González, Fuertes and other excellent poets who began writing in the fifties), *The Poetry of Discovery*, dispelled simplistic characterizations of this work and refined our notion of Spanish postwar poetry. The measure of linguistic deviation, once thought to decrease in proportion to the social commitment of the writer, had proved inadequate, leaving to contemporary and future critics the task of describing each postwar generation more accurately.

The third generation, mostly writers who have only recently turned forty, has not yet received the critical attention required for a clear understanding of their literary affinities. Since their poetry is relatively new, many literary scholars outside of Spain have not studied these texts in depth. Within Spain, the critical reaction to these poets has been polemic and in some instances oblique. The old political antagonisms, which pitted Left against Right and one region against another earlier in the century, reentered the literary arena, often disguised as aesthetic disagreement. Unbeknown to many readers, such factors as the poet's birthplace or political militancy have influenced the criteria of some anthologists. A particularly controversial anthology reached the public in 1970 when José María Castellet, a major Catalan critic, closely linked to the "social" poetry of the forties and fifties, published *Nueve novísimos poetas españoles* (Nine Very Recent Spanish Poets). His introductory comments and selection of poets, which portrayed Barcelona as the center of contemporary literary activity, provoked many critics to outrage. Some critics, particularly those on the Left, disliked Castellet's change of allegiance, from poetry that was politically and socially "correct" to poetry he had called "frivolous." Together, the anthology and the reactions to it, became the major literary phenomenon of the decade and may be associated irrevocably with the young poets who began writing in the late sixties and seventies.

I address the *novísimo* phenomenon in describing for the English-reading public the politicized literary milieu which existed in Spain when the poets of the third postwar generation began publishing. However, in selecting poets for this collection, I have looked beyond it to the richly diverse poems of four writers—Pere Gimferrer, Manuel Vázquez Montalbán, Guillermo Carnero, and Antonio Colinas—who are, I believe, among the best poets of their generation.

*K. P.*
*April 30, 1989*

# FOUR POSTMODERN POETS OF SPAIN

# INTRODUCTION

In 1966, a young, iconoclastic poet, Pere Gimferrer, won Spain's National Literary Prize for his first book of poems, *Arde el mar* (The Sea Is Burning). Two collections by poets close in age to Gimferrer appeared the following year: Guillermo Carnero's *Dibujo de la muerte* (Sketch of Death) and Manuel Vázquez Montalbán's *Una educación sentimental* (An Education on Feelings). Two years later, in 1969, another young poet, Antonio Colinas, published his first collections, *Poemas de la tierra y de la sangre* (Poems of the Earth and Blood) and *Preludios a una noche total* (Preludes to a Complete Night). Though richly diverse, these volumes shared a number of qualities which distinguished them from the waning neo-realist aesthetic of the forties and fifties and affirmed the revitalization of Spanish poetry undertaken at the end of that period by the second postwar generation (Brines, Rodríguez, Fuertes, González, and others). None of the four employed the testimonial posture or discursive style of "social" poetry, but focused rather on the personal world of the poet; and each expressed, with varying degrees of aestheticism and irrationalism, a content which aroused the interpretive capabilities of the reader.

The earliest anthologies featuring poets from the third postwar generation—collections that sometimes included poets from the previous generation—reached the market in 1967: Amelia Romero's *Doce jóvenes poetas españoles* (Twelve Young Spanish Poets) and Enrique Martín Pardo's *Antología de la joven poesía*

3

*española* (Anthology of Young Spanish Poets). In 1968, José Batlló's *Antología de la nueva poesía española* (Anthology of New Spanish Poetry) was the first to probe the literary affiliations of younger poets, specifically Gimferrer and Vázquez Montalbán, both of whom expressed an involvement with new trends and qualified their poetry as different from that of other poets in the anthology. Vázquez Montalbán stated: "There are 'new' Spanish poets who combine specific poetic influences and preparations with their new experiences, their new moral position, conditioned by an historical perspective different, for example, from the critical generation of the fifties" (Batlló 363).[1] Gimferrer also distinguished his generation from that of the fifties, and added, qualifying his statement as pertinent only to the first symptoms of a new movement: "Perhaps my generation will focus again on themes and devices which more urgent ethical concerns caused some, in a not so distant past, to disregard" (Batlló 340).[2]

From the beginning, before group affiliations existed, the new poetry came under attack. The changed perspective referred to by both Vázquez Montalbán and Gimferrer proved to be the major point of contention. The social realist aesthetic, which these and many other young poets reacted against, was so thoroughly infused with political doctrine that a departure from the aesthetic constituted a tacit rejection of the ideology. As Vázquez Montalbán observed: "Too many things are still mixed together in our [country], so mixed that I doubt that any aspect, no matter how small, of our national culture will ever become clear" (Batlló 363).[3]

This poet's statement indicates the nature of the polemic which would intensify in the seventies, creating major antagonisms and giving issue to numerous anthologies of poetry by young Spanish writers. Each anthologist attempted to define *joven poesía española* and in some cases to invalidate the appraisals of other anthologists involved in the same process. A new collection often stood as a rebuttal to some earlier one, by claiming to offer a more accurate list of poets and by attacking the premises and even motives of other anthologists. Each new anthology approximated a kind of literary *pronunciamiento* like those nineteenth and early twentieth century uprisings in which one faction after another proclaimed to have the correct and definitive answer.

4

The polemic heightened in 1970 with the publication of José María Castellet's *Nueve novísimos poetas españoles* (Nine Very Recent Spanish Poets). The anthologist, a prominent Catalan editor and essayist, chose nine poets whose verse signified, in his estimation, a complete divergence from the form and content of the "social" poetry of the forties and fifties. The first part of his introduction, which explored the break with the previous generation, focused on the stimulus of a changing social and political climate and attributed special importance to several facts: all of the *novísimos* were born after the Civil War, 1936–1939, and therefore had not been directly influenced by it. They had experienced the so-called "youth revolution" of the sixties; and, having received part of their education from the mass media, they had assimilated a type of "mythology" based on media-transmitted popular culture (12–26).

According to Castellet, these factors had given rise to a new sensibility with numerous stylistic manifestations: a disregard for the traditional literary forms, a preference for stream-of-consciousness or automatic writing, the use of elliptical techniques, such as syncopation and collage, and the introduction of exotic and artificial elements into the text. He characterized their verse in general terms as ambiguous, irrational, artificial and apparently frivolous (37–44). The communication of a paraphraseable statement, fundamental in "social" poetry, was no longer a concern for the *novísimos*, absorbed in exploring the imaginative possibilities of language.

The more dogmatic exponents of "social" poetry considered Castellet's prologue purely treasonous. In *Veinte años de poesía española* (Twenty Years of Spanish Poetry), published in 1960, Castellet had defended the social realist aesthetic of Spanish poetry in the forties and fifties. By turning away from his former posture, he was thought to have made an ideological as well as literary statement. Ironically, attacks also came from opponents on the Right who continued to harbor prejudices against Castellet based on his earlier commitment to "social" poetry (Grande 100). Given the divisive political and literary climate of 1970, the appropriation of *Nueve novísimos* as a target for adamant criticism is comprehensible, since some of the motivations for either attacking or supporting the anthology existed long before its publication. As Vázquez Montalbán's 1968 statement (quoted above) implies, the motivations behind any given criticism were often complex and not entirely literary. Clearly, political antagonisms were responsible in part for this widespread controversy, which Félix Grande described as a "ghost" haunting Spanish poetry: "For some the ghost is a book: *Nueve novísimos*. For others, the ghost is the ring of contempt or anger which that same book aroused in many of its abundant readers" (97).[4]

While many opponents disagreed with Castellet's prologue and his choice of poets, others objected to the new aesthetic per se, specifically its apparent rejection of an easily understood idiom. Some critics claimed that the *novísimo* poetry signified, in essence, a desertion of the realities of the common man (Grande 98). Those who insisted that art address itself to the needs of the proletariat considered the *novísimo* trend decadent and irrelevant. This kind of ideological quarrel led one *novísimo*, Vázquez Montalbán, to become temporarily estranged from his political group, the P.S.U.C. (Catalan Communist Party). A similar objection to the *novísimo* aesthetic came from the Equipo "Claraboya," a León-centered group, that called the *novísimo* phenomenon a "reflection of an incipient neo-capitalism already rooted in Catalonia" (Delgado et al. 17),[5] a statement suggesting a regional as well as political bias. Some others who objected to the aesthetic founded their arguments on strictly artistic criteria and expressed a preference for the *poesía última* (latest poetry) group —another name used for the second postwar generation—which had broken away from the direct testimonial approach of the "social" poets but still regarded poetry as a means of knowing reality.

Another set of objections, also with complex variations, challenged the status of the *novísimos* as the experimental vanguard in Spanish poetry. Some critics believed that such a status, unduly assigned to them by Castellet's anthology, belonged instead to other groups of poets, such as the exponents of *poesía concreta* (concrete poetry). Attacks of this kind also stemmed in part from extra-literary considerations. Castellet had offended the regional pride of certain poets and critics by claiming for the *novísimos* a major role in breaking with "social" poetry. This issue

6

was particularly sensitive for Andalusians, since several southern poets, such as Edmundo d'Ory, had espoused a different aesthetic during the neo-realist period. Manuel Urbano in his *Antología consultada de la nueva poesía andaluza (1963–1978)* (Consulting Anthology of New Andalusian Poetry), published in 1980, defended the contribution of Andalusian poets and objected in particular to Castellet's disregard of the Córdoba-based group, "Cántico." "Cántico," according to Urbano, had redirected Spanish poetry by taking up the symbolist approach, used by some of Spain's best modern poets—Bécquer, Lorca, and others (22).

Although the *novísimo* phenomenon, both the anthology and the reactions to it, skewed our view of Spanish poetry in the seventies, making the task of critics interested in a more purely aesthetic evaluation more laborious, on the positive side, it led to a proliferation of anthologies of poetry by young—often unpublished—writers. Between 1970 and 1982, more than twenty anthologies featured the works of recent Spanish poets, and an additional number dealt with recent poets from a particular region. The most important of these include Enrique Martín Pardo's *Nueva poesía española* (1970), Antonio Prieto's *Espejo del amor y de la muerte: antología de poesía española última* (1971), Florencio Martínez Ruiz's *Nueva poesía española: antología crítica: segunda generación de postguerra, 1955–1970* (1971), and Agustín Delgado's *Equipo "Claraboya": Teoría y poemas* (1971). These were followed by Joaquín González Muela's *La nueva poesía española* (1973), José Batlló's *Poetas españoles poscontemporáneos* (1974), Fernando Millán and Jesús García Sánchez's *La escritura en libertad* (1975), Víctor Pozanco's *Nueve poetas del resurgimiento* (1976), Concepción G[arcía] Moral and Rosa María Pereda's *Joven poesía española: Antología* (1979), a second by Víctor Pozanco, entitled *Segunda antología del resurgimiento* (1980), José Luis García Martín's *Las voces y los ecos* (1980), and Elena de Jongh Rossel's *Florilegium: Poesía última española* (1982). Although Fanny Rubio and José Luis Falcó's *Poesía española contemporánea: 1939–1980* (1981) included poetry representing several postwar generations, the lengthy section dedicated to the seventies constitutes still another anthology of *joven poesía española;* Falcó's introductory chapter on this generation is one of the more complete surveys written to date. G. L. Solner's *Poesía española hoy* (1982) also devoted a substantial portion to the third postwar generation.

No single anthology adequately defined this third postwar generation, but each expanded the public's knowledge of these writers. All together, more than seventy poets were represented in the major anthologies published between 1970 and 1982. Fourteen of these appeared in three or more anthologies. In order of age, with their birthplaces, they include Manuel Vázquez Montalbán (Barcelona, 1939), Antonio Martínez Sarrión (Albacete, 1939), José María Alvarez (Cartagena, 1942), Antonio Carvajal (Granada, 1943), Félix de Azúa (Barcelona, 1944), José-Miguel Ullán (Salamanca, 1944), Pere Gimferrer (Barcelona, 1945), José Luis Jover (Cuenca, 1946), Antonio Colinas (León, 1946), Jenaro Taléns (Cadiz, 1946), Guillermo Carnero (Valencia, 1947), Leopoldo María Panero (Madrid, 1948), Jaime Siles (Valencia, 1951) and Luis Antonio de Villena (Madrid, 1951).

Since the publication of *Nueve novísimos poetas españoles*, a number of writers have offered less controversial and perhaps more accurate analyses of the works of poets who began publishing in the mid-sixties. Three insightful studies which treat the common traits of these writers are José Olivio Jiménez's *Diez años de poesía española* (*Ten Years of Spanish Poetry*) 1972, his prologue to Antonio Colinas's collected poetry (1982; 1984), and Carlos Bousoño's prologue to the complete works of Guillermo Carnero, *Ensayo de una teoría de la visión* (Testing a Theory of Vision) 1979. Jiménez discovered a commonality in the poetry of the seventies which took into account Colinas, Antonio Carvajal, Luis Antonio de Villena, Jaime Siles and several others excluded from the *novísimos* (Prologue 12–13). Bousoño particularized the subjectivism of this generation within the Romantic spectrum by discovering in their world view a rejection of "rationalistic reason" ("razón racionalista" 16), reason which relies on generalization and abstraction rather than individual experience (16).[6] Nevertheless, no other study or anthology rivals Castellet's in creating "a delicious epocal flavor" ("un delicioso sabor de época;" García Martín 34), relating many social and cultural realities of the late sixties with some of Spain's young poets. His prologue, like many of the poems, recreates the mentality of a generation by means of a collage of names and titles: motion pictures of the forties and fifties, Superman and Flash Gordon comics, Agatha Christie, Marilyn Monroe, Aretha Franklin, Bertrand Russell, Che Guevara, Allen Ginsberg, Marshall McLuhan, Umberto Eco and Roland Barthes. Members of that generation both in Spain and abroad may perhaps see a vision of themselves, at that time, in Henry James' character Hyacinth Robinson, whose self-portrait Castellet chose as an epigraph to the anthology:

> I am one of many thousands of young men of my class—you know, I suppose, what that is—in whose brains certain ideas are fermenting. There is nothing original about me at all. I am very young and very ignorant; it's only a few months since I began to talk of the possibility of a social revolution with men who have considered the whole ground much more than I have done. I'm a mere particle in the immensity of the people. All I pretend to is my good faith, and a great desire that justice shall be done. (161)[7]

## PERE GIMFERRER

*Barcelona, 1945*

# PERE

# GIMFERRER

Pere Gimferrer was born in Barcelona in 1945. Although Catalan was his first language, he published his early verse in Castilian and, by the age of twenty-one, had won Spain's prestigious National Literary Prize. In his *ars poetica* for *Nueve novísimos poetas españoles,* a collection edited by Castellet but largely inspired by Gimferrer, he summarized the essential elements of his artistic development: a solitary childhood marked by a precocious dedication to reading; friendships in late adolescence with youths of similar cultural sensibilities, some of whom were also included in *Nueve novísimos;* a disinterest in established literary tastes and a preference for exotic, dissident or unusual writers such as Kafka, Faulkner, Proust, and James; a passion for jazz and, above all, American motion pictures of the thirties and forties, the images of which would fill the pages of his early poetry ("Poética" 155–58).[1]

In addition to the baroque poets, the Hispanic Modernists and the Generation of 1927, Gimferrer read and learned from numerous foreign sources, including Saint-John Perse, Pound, and Eliot. At nineteen he discovered the work of the Mexican poet and theoretician Octavio Paz and initiated an exchange of ideas through correspondence, which together with his friendship and correspondence with Vicente Aleixandre, would be his major literary associations before the age of forty. Aleixandre encouraged him to publish his first book of poems; and when Aleixandre died in 1985, Gimferrer accepted his chair in the Royal Language Academy.

As Gimferrer explained in his 1970 *ars poetica*, he composed his early verse with jazz or radio music playing in the background and with cinematographic images passing before his mind's eye. In his first volume, *Arde el mar* (The Sea Is Burning) 1966, he experimented with automatic writing; in later volumes, *La muerte en Beverly Hills* (Death in Beverly Hills) 1968, and *Extraña fruta* (Strange Fruit), published in *Poemas 1963–1969* (1969), his writing became more conscious, more deliberate. During this early period he began cultivating musicality, fragmentation, and the metapoetic theme, which would become the essential ingredients of his style. He learned to combine the classical rhythms of the Renaissance hendecasyllabic line, which lent a traditional and formalistic flavor to his poetry, with an elliptical style reminiscent of modern writers such as Eliot. Gimferrer was able to blend such seemingly disparate elements so that the fragments of his discourse, derived from numerous and varied sources, were held together in poetic unity by the sound and rhythm of the line.

The persona of these early poems, young, Romantic and faltering, returns repeatedly to a set of unanswered questions which he addresses *to* himself *about* himself. He is very much like the protagonist of Robert Penn Warren's *Band of Angels;* possibly the film version of the novel, which Gimferrer had seen, was present in his mind as he wrote. He uses Warren's title for the next to the last poem in *Arde el mar,* although for its thematic relevance, it could have been a title for a number of poems in the anthology. None of these compositions refers specifically to the novel, but several recall the first glimpse of Warren's Amantha Starr engaged in a strikingly similar ritual of self-analysis:

"Oh, who am I?" For so long that was, you might say, the cry of my heart. . . . And then, sometimes, there would come into my head the picture of a grassy place. . . . I can never describe this place too clearly, even to myself, the way you can't describe a dream. When you try to tell somebody about a dream, you find in the telling that you are simply having another dream, and different, and even the feeling of the old one changes. . . . But there was, in sober fact, a grassy place, no dream. . . . Sometimes this real spot and the spot of my imagination, of my dream . . . seem to become the same spot. . . . Why, then, do the two images, with such poignant excitement, sometimes merge in my heart? (3-4)

The personae of poems like "Ode to Venice While Watching the Sea on a Stage" and "First Vision of March" (both from *Arde el mar*) experience this same bifurcation of self and setting; standing in one spot—Venice, a garden, a cloister—he remembers the same spot at a moment lost in time and asks which one is true. Also, the nostalgia, or sadness, the loss of self and experience, become in the retelling another reality, or unreality. In writing about himself, then, the young poet must come to grips with several "selves": the one who lives and writes in the present, the one whom he remembers, and the one who comes to life in the poem. The contemplation of the poematic self and its comparison with the other selves makes these poems metapoetic, since it leads the poet to examine in the poem the reality which the poem has contrived.

In 1970, Gimferrer published *Els miralls* (*The Mirrors*), his first volume in Catalan.[2] The shift from one language to another brought with it stylistic changes. It is very likely that the poet's desire for renovation partially motivated the change to Catalan. Gimferrer recognized that, notwithstanding the similarities between his mother tongue and Castilian, each language reflects its own literary tradition; likewise, each possesses its particular mechanical advantages for imagery, suggestibility, and rhythm. While exploring the possibilities of a different language, he refocused his poetic vision and began to create verse which differed in several ways from his first poems in Castilian: the hendecasyllabic line gives way to freer versification; although fragmentation is still prevalent, the flow of ideas takes on an apparent logic; and the treatment of poetry as a theme, earlier tied to the problem of self, becomes a more deliberate analysis of the representational limits of language.

Also, as Gimferrer has grown older, his poetry has become less personal and more abstract. His early preoccupation with his own existence later on yields to an interest in experiences external to himself; and later still, he peers deeply into essences of a cosmic order. The poems that I have chosen for this anthology exemplify such an evolution from *Arde el mar* to *Apariciones y otros poemas* (Apparitions and Other Poems) 1982, his last volume translated to Castilian. The first four poems, all from the former volume, are nostalgic recollections of childhood and early manhood. By *Els miralls*, represented by the next two poems, a more objective, narrative voice has taken the place of the earlier, Romantic persona. For the most part, he stands at a distance, intervening occasionally to comment on the poem in question or to expound on the language-reality problem. With *Apariciones*, represented by the last poem, Gimferrer arrives at his most philosophical posture, and the personal experiences of the poet, as man or writer, give way to meditations on night, space, and the vegetable kingdom.

In spite of the differences which come to light when poems from various volumes are compared, what Gimferrer has said of other writers, that the poet always writes the same poem, can also be said of his own work. Although his technique evolves, his basic definition of poetry does not change: a poem is not a discourse on an idea but a picture concealed in words. In fact, Gimferrer would have us believe that it is the poet's *modus operandi* to avoid discourse. He has stated, quoting Mallarmé, "poetry isn't made with ideas but with words," and, quoting Barthes, "writers are not those who have something to say but something to write" (Guerrero Martín 14).[3] Although it may be a natural tendency to look for meaning in what one reads—the kind of meaning that answers the question "What does it say?"—Gimferrer's poetry requires a different kind of reading. What he brings to the poem are the images which his senses knew, for him the most extricable part of an experience. Very little abstraction enters the poem, even in his later meditations, which, like the early verse, rely heavily on the communicative power of images. Instead of developing a theme or expounding an idea rationally, he reproduces the mystical, unlimitable knowledge of a feeling, a feeling which he senses in a merging of images, first in his eye and then on the page.

His vision is supremely resistant to conceptualization. There are thoughts and narrative elements in his poetry, but neither a philosophy nor a story emerges. The individual segments of a poem, which might have developed into a statement or a narrative, function instead as indeterminate parts of a hidden picture which the reader must discover for himself. In the poem, "Snares," from *Poesía 1970–1977*, the poet gives us some indication of what to expect when confronting the difficulties of a poem:

> This poem is
> a series of snares: for the
> reader and for the
> copy editor
> and for
> the publisher.
>
>         In other words,
> they haven't told me either
> what's in the snares, because
> that would be like telling me the picture
> in the tapestry, and that
> is exactly what James teaches us cannot
> be done.
>
>            (41)[4]

# POEMS

# ◆ ODA A VENECIA ANTE EL MAR DE LOS TEATROS

*Las copas falsas, el veneno y la calavera*
*de los teatros.*

GARCÍA LORCA

*A Joaquín Marco*

Tiene el mar su mecánica como el amor sus símbolos.
Con qué trajín se alza una cortina roja
o en esta embocadura de escenario vacío
suena un rumor de estatuas, hojas de lirio, alfanjes,
palomas que descienden y suavemente pósanse.
Componer con chalinas un ajedrez verdoso.
El moho en mi mejilla recuerda el tiempo ido
y una gota de plomo hierve en mi corazón.
Llevé la mano al pecho, y el reloj corrobora
la razón de las nubes y su velamen yerto.
Asciende una marea, rosas equilibristas
sobre el arco voltaico de la noche en Venecia
aquel año de mi adolescencia perdida,
mármol en la Dogana como observaba Pound
y la masa de un féretro en los densos canales.
Id más allá, muy lejos aún, hondo en la noche,
sobre el tapiz del Dux, sombras entretejidas,
príncipes o nereidas que el tiempo destruyó.
Qué pureza un desnudo o adolescente muerto
en las inmensas salas del recuerdo en penumbra.
¿Estuve aquí? ¿Habré de creer que éste he sido
y éste fue el sufrimiento que punzaba mi piel?
Qué frágil era entonces, y por qué. ¿Es más verdad,
copos que os diferís en el parque nevado,
el que hoy así acoge vuestro amor en el rostro
o aquél que allá en Venecia de belleza murió?
Las piedras vivas hablan de un recuerdo presente.

20

# ◆ ODE TO VENICE WHILE WATCHING THE SEA ON A STAGE

*The phony cups, the poison and the skull on the stage.*

FEDERICO GARCÍA LORCA

To Joaquín Marco

The sea has its mechanics as love its symbols.
With what ado a red curtain rises
or, on this empty stage, sound
the murmuring of statues, lily petals, cutlasses,
doves flying down and perching smoothly.
To weave with scarves a greenish chessboard.
The rust on my cheek brings to mind times gone by
and a drop of lead boils in my heart.
I brought my hand to my breast, and the clock confirms
the rationale of clouds and their petrified sails.
The tide rises, roses walking the tightrope
on the voltaic arc of that night in Venice
the year of my lost adolescence,
marble in the Dogana as Pound observed
and the lump of a coffin on the dense canals.
Go on, still much further, deep into the night,
against the Dux's tapestry, interwoven shadows,
princes or nereids destroyed by time.
What purity a nude or dead adolescent
in the vast halls of penumbral memories.
Was I ever here? Must I believe that I was this one
and that this was the suffering that pricked my skin?
How frail I was then, and why. Which is truer,
flakes differing on the snow-covered park,
the one who now receives your love on his face thus
or that one who died of beauty there in Venice?
The live stones speak of a present memory.

Como la vena insiste sus conductos de sangre,
va, viene y se remonta nuevamente al planeta
y así la vida expande en batán silencioso,
el pasado se afirma en mí a esta hora incierta.
Tanto he escrito, y entonces tanto escribí. No sé
si valía la pena o la vale. Tú, por quien
es más cierta mi vida, y vosotros, que oís
en mi verso otra esfera, sabréis, su signo o arte.
Dilo, pues, o decidlo, y dulcemente acaso
mintáis a mi tristeza. Noche, noche en Venecia
va para cinco años, ¿cómo tan lejos? Soy
el que fui entonces, sé tensarme y ser herido
por la pura belleza como entonces, violín
que parte en dos el aire de una noche de estío
cuando el mundo no puede soportar su ansiedad
de ser bello. Lloraba yo, acodado al balcón
como en un mal poema romántico, y el aire
promovía disturbios de humo azul y alcanfor.
Bogaba en las alcobas, bajo el granito húmedo,
un arcángel o sauce o cisne o corcel de llama
que las potencias últimas enviaban a mi sueño.
                                        Lloré, lloré, lloré.
¿Y cómo pudo ser tan hermoso y tan triste?
Agua y frío rubí, transparencia diabólica
grababan en mi carne un tatuaje de luz.
Helada noche, ardiente noche, noche mía
como si hoy la viviera! Es doloroso y dulce
haber dejado atrás la Venecia en que todos
para nuestro castigo fuimos adolescentes
y perseguirnos hoy por las salas vacías
en ronda de jinetes que disuelve un espejo
negando, con su doble, la realidad de este poema.

As a vein presses on its blood conduits,
it goes back and forth and soars again to the planet
and thus life expands, milling away in silence,
the past takes hold of me at this uncertain hour.
I've written so much, and wrote so much then.
I don't know if it was or is worthwhile. You
on whose account my life rings truer, and you all,
who hear in my verse a different sphere, will know
its sign and artifice. Say it, then, or all of you, maybe
you will gently fool my sadness. Night, night in Venice
almost five years now. How come so far off? I am
the one that I was then, I can string up and be hurt
by sheer beauty like then, a violin
that splits in two the air of a summer night
when the world cannot bear its passionate yearning
to be beautiful. I was weeping, my elbow on the balcony
like a bad romantic poem, and the air
caused disturbances of blue smoke and camphor.
Through the alcoves, under the damp granite
an archangel or willow or swan or charger sailed in flames
sent to my dreams by the ultimate powers.
                                        I wept and wept and wept.
How could it possibly be so beautiful, so sad?
Water and cold ruby, diabolical transparence
were marking in my flesh a tattoo of light.
Cold night, sweltering night, my very own night
as if I were living it now! It is painful and sweet
to have left behind the Venice where we all
for our own punishment were adolescents
and to chase one another, now, through the empty halls
in a round of horsemen which a mirror dissolves,
denying, with its double, the reality of this poem.

*Translated by Manuel López*


*The Sea Is Burning* (1966)

# ◆ PRIMERA VISIÓN DE MARZO

## I

¡Transustanciación!
                    El mar, como un jilguero,
vivió en las enramadas. Sangre, dime,
repetida en los pulsos,
que es verdad el color de la magnolia, el grito
del ánade a lo lejos, la espada en mi cintura
como estatua o dios muerto, bailarín de teatro.
¿No me mentís? Sabría
apenas alzar lámparas, biombos,
horcas de nieve o llama en esta vida
tan ajena y tan mía, así interpuesta
como en engaño o arte, mas por quién
o por qué misericordia?
Yo fui el que estuvo en este otro jardín
ya no cierto, y el mar hecho ceniza
fingió en mis ojos su estremecimiento
y su vibrar de aletas, súbitamente estáticas
cuando el viento cambió y otras voces venían
—¿desde aquella terraza?—en vez de las antiguas,
color de helecho y púrpura, armadura en el agua.
Tanto poema escrito en unos meses,
tanta historia sin nombre ni color ni sonido,
tanta mano olvidada como musgo en la arena,
tantos días de invierno que perdí y reconquisto
sobre este mismo círculo y este papel morado.
No hay pantalla o visera, no hay trasluz
ni éstas son sombras de linterna mágica:
cal surca el rostro del guerrero, roen
urracas o armadillos el encaje en los claustros.

# ◆ FIRST VISION OF MARCH

### I

Transubstantiation!
             The sea, like a linnet,
lived in the branches of trees. Tell me, blood,
pulsing in my veins,
that the color of the magnolia is true, the call
of the eider in the distance, the sword at my waist
like a statue or dead god, theatrical dancer.
Aren't you deceiving me? I would scarcely have known
how to raise up lamps, folding screens,
gallows made of snow or flame in this life
so far from me and so much mine, interposed
as by art or deception, but by whom
or by what mercy?
I was the one in this other garden
no longer certain, and the sea, turned to ashes,
acted out its trembling in my eyes,
its fluttering of fins, suddenly ecstatic
when the wind changed and other voices came
—from that terrace over there?—instead of the old ones,
color of fern and purple, armor in the water.
So much poetry written in a matter of months,
so much fiction without a name, color or sound,
so many hands forgotten like moss on the sand,
so many days of winter I lost and reconquer now
on this same circle and violet paper.
There is no screen or visor, no transverse light
and these are not the shadows of a magic lamp:
lime furrows the face of the warrior,
magpies or armadillos gnaw the cloister railings.

Yo estuve una mañana, casi hurtada
al presuroso viaje: tamizaban la luz
sus calados de piedra, y las estatuas
—soñadas desde niño—imponían su fulgor inanimado
como limón o esfera al visitante.
Visión, sueño yo mismo,
contemplaba la estatua en un silencio
hecho sólo de memoria, cristal o piedra tallada
pero frío en las yemas, ascendiendo
como un lento amarillo sobre el aire en tensión.
Hacia otro, hacia otra
vida, desde mi vida, en el común
artificio o rutina con que se hace un poema,
un largo poema y su gruesa artillería,
sin misterio, ni apenas
este sordo conjuro que organiza palabras o fluctúa
de una a otra, vivo en su contradicción.
Interminablemente, mar,
supe de ti: gaviotas a lo lejos
se volvían espuma, y ella misma
era una larga línea donde alcanzan los ojos: unidad. Y en el
    agua
van y vienen tritones y quimeras, pero es más fácil
decir que vivo en ella y que mi historia
se relata en su pálido lenguaje.
Pentagrama marino, arquitectónico,
qué lejano a este instante muerto bajo la mesa,
al sol en la pecera y el ámbar en los labios,
a la lengua de cáñamo que de pronto ayer tuve.
Interiormente llamo o ilumino
esferas del pasado y me sé tan distinto
como se puede ser siendo uno mismo y pienso
en el mejor final para este raro poema
empezado al azar una tarde de marzo.

I was there on a morning, nearly fettered
to the hasty trip: eyelets of stone
filtered the light, and the statues
—dreamed about since childhood—imposed their inanimate
  splendor,
like a lemon or sphere, upon the visitor.
Vision, a dream myself,
I watched the statue in silence
made entirely of memory, glass or chiseled stone,
but with cold fingertips, rising up
like a slow yellow above the air in tension.
Towards another, towards another
life, from my life, in the common
craft or routine a poem is made of,
a long poem and its heavy artillery,
without mystery, not even
this silent incantation that orders words or fluctuates
from one to another, alive in its contradiction.
I've known you interminably, sea:
seagulls in the distance
were turning to foam, and it, in turn, was a long line
as far as the eyes can see: unity. And chimeras
and tritons come and go in the water, but it's easier
to say that I live in it and my story
is told in its pale language.
Marine, architectonic pentagram,
so far away from this moment dead beneath the table,
from the sun in the fishbowl and the amber of my lips,
from the hemp tongue I suddenly got yesterday.
Inside me, I beckon or light up
spheres from the past and I know I'm as different
as one can be, being oneself, and I wonder
how best to end this unusual poem
begun by chance one afternoon in March.

## II

La tarde me asaltaba como una primavera
en Arezzo, y yo cedía al repertorio
de emociones y usos de poeta: deidades
se materializaban a mi voz, faunos ígneos
amenazaban cada gruta, sombras
de mí mismo me esperaban bajo el tapial de álamos.
(Todavía no he hablado, ni lo haré,
de otros prodigios, alcotán o ninfa Egeria,
clase de francés a mis doce años o recuerdos de una guerra
    no vivida,
primeras horas con Montaigne o inútiles lecciones de solfeo,
minotauro de Picasso y poesía entre mis apuntes, toda una
    memoria abolida
por el silencio encapuchado de esta tarde.)
Penitente el jardín, las hojas ciegas
amarilleaban obstinadamente.
                Sin duda vine a esto,
y no llamado por un rito o mística
revelación; sabiendo, y aceptando,
que nada iba a hallar sino en mí mismo.
                  Así el jardín es otra
imagen o rodeo, como al final de un súbito pasillo
la luz se abre y el balcón llamea,
ignorado hasta entonces; o más bien
la pausa entre relámpago y relámpago,
cuando en la oscuridad todo es espera
y de pronto llegó (¿pero era esto?)
                  Luces
inquietan el jardín, como de balneario
—un quinteto en la pérgola, té, gravilla—donde aún es
    posible
reconocerse, aquél, bajo los sauces tártaros,
y estar allí sin que nadie lo sepa,
como uno que viajó consigo mismo en el avión, entre
    brumas neerlandesas,

## II

The afternoon fell upon me like a spring
in Arezzo, and I gave way to the repertory
of emotions and devices of the poet: deities
appeared at my word, fiery fauns
threatened every grotto, shadows
of myself were waiting under a frame of poplars.
(I haven't spoken yet, nor will I,
of other portents, the falcon or the nymph Egeria,
French class when I was twelve or memories of a war I
    hadn't lived,
first hours with Montaigne or useless lessons of sol-fa,
Picasso's minotaur and poetry in with my notes, the whole
    memory abolished
by the hooded silence of the afternoon.)
Once the garden was repentant, the blind leaves
obstinately changed to yellow.
                      Doubtless, I came to this,
not beckoned by a rite or mystic
revelation; but knowing, and accepting,
that I would find nothing if not inside myself.
                    So the garden is another
image or winding round, as at the end of an unexpected
    passage
light enters and the balcony flames forth,
unseen until then; or perhaps
the pause between one flash of lightning and another,
when, in the darkness, there's only the waiting
and suddenly it came—but was it this?
                      Lights
disturb the garden, the resort kind
—a quintet on the roof garden, tea, small gravel—where you
still can see yourself, that one over there, under the Tartarian
    willows,
and be there without anyone finding out,
like someone who rode with himself in a plane, through
    Dutch fog,

y aún hoy lo ignora.
Fácil, fácil conquista, marzo y árboles rojos.
Surtidor el unánime, tened piedad de mí.

## III

¡Con qué tenacidad
insiste la columna!
Serpiente o mármol o marfil
en el silencio ovalado de la plaza
impone su ascensión: oro o musgo que crece,
sal y rumor de luces submarinas.
Medallones del sol, a plomo sobre el aire,
se fijan en el muro y su estertor calcáreo:
arden, mueren, desmienten
una verticalidad hecha de sombra.
                                    Veo
con otros ojos, no los míos, esta plaza
soñada en otros tiempos, hoy vivida,
con un susurro de algas al oído
viniendo de muy lejos.
                          Atención:
bajo el viento de marzo la plaza en trance vibra
como un tambor de piedra.
Mar o libro de horas,
se trata de ordenar estos datos dispersos.

## IV

Ordenar estos datos es tal vez poesía.
El cristal delimita, entre lluvia y visillos,
la inmóvil fosforescencia del jardín.
Un aro puede arder entre la nieve bárbara.
Ved al aparecido y su jersey azul.
Así puedo deciros
esto o aquello, aproximarme apenas

and doesn't know it even now.
Easy, an easy conquest, March and red trees.
Giver of all Gifts, have mercy on me.


## III

How tenaciously
the column persists!
Serpent or marble or ivory
in the oval silence of the square
imposes its ascension: gold or growing moss,
the salt and sound of underwater lights.
Medallions of the sun, lying flat on the air,
settle on the wall and its calcareous breathing:
they burn, die and contradict
a verticalness made of shadow.
                                        I see
this square with other eyes than mine,
imagined at other times, lived today,
with a whisper of algae at my ear
coming from very far away.
                                        Listen:
beneath the winds of March, the square, entranced, vibrates
like a stone drum.
Sea or book of hours,
it's a question of putting these random facts in order.


## IV

Putting these facts in order is perhaps poetry.
Between curtains and rain, the glass delimits
the still phosphorescence of the garden.
A hoop can burn in the fierce snow.
See who's appeared and his blue sweater.
So I can tell you
this or that, barely approach

a la verdad inaprensible, como
buscando el equilibrio de una nota indecisa
que aún no es y ya pasó, qué pura.
Violines o atmósferas.
                    Color muralla, el aire
proyectando más aire se hace tiempo y espacio.
                              Así nosotros
movemos nuestras lanzas ante el brumoso mar
y son ciertas las luces, el sordo roce de espuelas y correaje,
los ojos del alazán y tal vez algo más, como en un buen
    cuadro.

the inconceivable truth, as if
searching for the harmony of an unsteady note
which isn't yet but already happened: so pure.
Violins or atmospheres.
                         A wall color, the air,
projecting more air, becomes time and space.
                                        So we
move our lances before the misty sea
and the lights are true, the silent graze of spurs and gear,
the eyes of the sorrel horse and perhaps something more, like
   in a good painting.


*The Sea Is Burning* (1966)

## ◆ BAND OF ANGELS

Un jazmín invertido me contiene,
una campana de agua, un rubí líquido
disuelto en sombras, una aguja de aire
y gas dormido, una piel de carnero
tendida sobre el mundo, una hoja de álamo
inmensamente dulce, cuanto puede
vegetal y callado remansarse
sobre nuestras cabezas, y la sien
y los labios y el dorso de la mano
ungir de luz:
          Tú llegas.
                    Mía, mía
como el árbol del cielo de noviembre,
la lluvia del que en sus cristales óyela
y piensa en ella, el mar de su eco lóbrego,
el viento de la cueva donde expira
y se sume, pasado el planisferio,
la luz de su reflejo en un estanque,
el astro de su luz, del tiempo el hombre
que lo vivió y luchó para ganarlo,
ganando aquél, del silencio la música
que un instante ha cesado y se retiene
para volcarse luego, un solo río,
una sola correinte de oro en pie,
inmóvil y cambiante, tal el signo
de la centella en el recuerdo, cuando
la pensamos y fue, sobre la tapia
en cal de nuestra infancia, un aro roto,
y aquel fulgor estremeciendo el aire,
caliente en las mejillas, glacial luego,
cuando la lluvia en chaparrón nos vence

## ◆ BAND OF ANGELS

A jasmine upside down holds me,
a bell of water, liquid ruby
dissolved in shadows, needle of air
and dormant gas, a goat's hide spread
upon the world, a poplar leaf
supremely sweet, and all that's silent
and vegetal finds repose
upon our heads or anoints with light
our temples, our lips and the
backs of our hands:
                        You arrive.
                              Mine, mine
as the tree belongs to the November sky,
the rain to the one whose window it hits
making him think, the sea to its dark echo,
the wind to the cave that receives and
consumes it, past the planisphere,
the light to its reflection on a pond,
the star to its light, to time the man
who lived and strived to overcome it, but
was overcome; to silence the music
that having stopped for an instant, hangs suspended
and then bursts out, one river,
a single stream of gold standing,
motionless and changing, just as the sign
belongs to the spark of remembrance, when
we thought it and it was, on the whitewashed
mudwall of our childhood, a broken hoop,
and that splendor shattering the air,
hot on our cheeks, then bitter cold,
when the pouring rain defeats us

y vence a nuestra infancia:
                              toda mía
como esa infancia que no tuve, el ruido
de una máquina al coser, tarde perlada
de cansancio, cortinas fantasmales,
unánime el pasillo hacia el balcón
y la calle entre rejas, un perfil
desconocido, el mío, y en sus ojos
otra luz de leyenda, un mundo, salas,
caminos, rosas, montes, arboledas,
tapices, cuadros, parques de granito,
abanicos abiertos, tumba abierta
con un ángel de mármol, tumba abierta
con coronas y versos, tumba abierta
de un niño, tumba oscura, aún mi pelo
rizado estaba, tumba abierta al cierzo
y la lluvia de otoño, verdes eran
ya mis ojos, en mi boca había un lirio,
tumba abierta de barro removido,
paletadas de estiércol en los ojos
de un niño, tumba abierta, venid todos,
murió en noviembre y llueve en su piel blanca,
llueve con la dulzura del otoño
y el dolor de la infancia que no tuve
y hoy sueño para ti,
                              pues eres mía,
mía como lo más mío de mí mismo.

Yo te he esperado años, y no importa
(no debiera importar) que sin tu luz
permanezca unas horas, escribiendo
poemas al azar, mientras te sé
con otras gentes—¿tú, la que me sueño,
o la que eres?—ida, ajena, en este
país tan tuyo de metal y sombra
donde no puedo entrar, en este tiempo
vivido sólo por y para ti,
el tiempo de la sala de concierto

and defeats our childhood:
                              all mine
like the childhood I never had, the noise
of a sewing machine, afternoon pearly
with exhaustion, spectral drapes,
the corridor undistracted to the balcony
and the street through the grating, a strange
profile, mine, and in its eyes
another legendary glimmer, a world, halls,
roads, roses, forest hills, groves,
tapestries, paintings, granite parks,
fans flung open, open tomb
like a marble angel, open tomb
with wreathes and verses, open tomb
of a child, somber tomb, my hair was
still curly, tomb proudly open to the north wind
and to the autumn rains, my eyes already
green, a lily in my mouth,
open tomb of broken mud bricks,
shovelfuls of manure on the eyes
of a child, open tomb, everyone come,
he died in November and rain falls on his white skin,
the rain falls with the sweetness of autumn
and the grief of a childhood I never had
and which I now dream for you,
                                        because you're mine,
mine as my innermost self, my very own.

I've waited for you long, it makes no difference
(it shouldn't make a difference) if without
your light I keep on writing poems
at random, while I know for sure that you're
with other people—you, the one I dream,
or the one you are?—gone, a stranger in this
land all yours of metal and shadow
which I'm not allowed to enter, this time
lived just because of you and for your sake,
the days of the concert hall

donde entraste aquel día, y bruscamente
te vi partir, sabiéndome a tu lado
y queriéndome aún, mas desde lejos,
donde imposible no sonó mi paso
ni mi respiración de amor llegaba
a tus cabellos, desde el centro mismo
de la otra vida, el corazón magnético
que envolvía en un círculo, hacia arriba,
sala y rostros y música y a ti.
No debiera importar que no te tenga
de este modo en las horas que tú vives
lejos de mí, fiel a tu vida propia,
para luego en la luz de amor transida
de mis ojos reconocerte en mí
y latir al unísono los pulsos,
astros, flores y frutos del amor;
no debiera importarme, mas no sé
dar al olvido tantos años muertos,
tanta belleza inútil, pues no vista
ni gozada contigo, tanto instante
que no sentí, pues no sentí a tu lado,
toda mi vida antes de abrirme a ti:
este jardín, esta terraza misma,
el vientre tibio de la noche fuera,
las ubres ciegas del pasado, el agua
latiendo al fondo de un poema, el fuego
crepitando en la cumbre de un poema,
la cruz donde confluye el elemento,
el círculo o conjuro cabalístico,
la pezuña del diablo, los ardides
que con mi amor fabrican poesía
como metal innoble.
          Veo el claustro
ya en silencio a esta hora de la tarde,
mágico en la distancia y la memoria,
arropado de sombras indecisas,
y tú saliendo, tu cabello suave
que ahuyenta las brujas, tu mirada

you walked into that day, and I saw you leave
abruptly, feeling me near you,
loving me still, even more from afar
where my steps could not possibly be heard
and my breath of love could have never reached
your tresses, from the very same center
of the other life, the magnetic heart
that embraced, in a spiral moving upward,
the hall, the faces, the music and you.
It shouldn't make a difference then if when
you're far away wrapped up in your own life
I cannot have—but soon you see yourself
in the sad love light of my eyes,
our pulses beating to the rhythm of—
the stars, the flowers, and the fruits of love;
it shouldn't make a difference, but I can't
yield all those dead years to oblivion
so much useless beauty, since not seen
or shared with you, so many moments
I never felt because I was without you,
all that I lived, before I opened myself
to you: this garden, this very terrace,
the warm womb of the night out there,
the blind udders of the past, the water
beating in the depths of a poem, the fire
crackling at the peak of a poem, the
cross where the elements meet, the circle
or the cabalistic incantation,
the hoof of the devil, the stratagems
which with my love make poetry
like base metal.
                    I see the cloister
silent now at this evening hour,
magic in the distance, in my memory
clothed in indecisive shadows,
and you emerging, your silky tresses
that drive away the witches, and your eyes

vertida en algo más allá de ti,
la astral fosforescencia de tus dientes,
el hielo dulce y terso de tus labios,
todas las dalias que en tu piel expiran
y en cada pliegue de tu cuerpo, y toda
la piedad que tus manos me conceden.
Irreductiblemente, ¿cómo ves
al que te espera, con tus ojos puros?
Supiera esto, y tú serías mía,
y al esperarte ahora, en esta tarde
que existe sólo porque existes tú,
la luz que confabula este poema
incendiaría nuestra soledad.
Ven hasta mí, belleza silenciosa,
talismán de un planeta no vivido,
imagen del ayer y del mañana
que influye en las mareas y los versos;
ven hasta mí y tus labios y tus ojos
y tus manos me salven de morir.

casting a glance at something beyond,
the astral phosphorescence of your teeth,
the sweet, smooth ice of your lips,
all the dahlias perishing on your skin
and in every fold of your body, and all
the piety that your hands can give me.
Irreducibly, how do you see the one
that waits for you, with your pure eyes?
If I could know this, you would be mine,
and as I wait for you this evening
which is real only because you are real,
the light that plots this poem
would set our loneliness on fire.
Come to me, silent Beauty,
talisman of an unexperienced planet,
image of yesterday and tomorrow
that flows over tides and verses;
come to me and may your lips and your eyes
and your hands save me from dying.

*Translated by Manuel López*

*The Sea Is Burning* (1966)

## ◆ EL ARPA EN LA CUEVA

Ardía el bosque silenciosamente.
Las nubes del otoño proseguían
su cacería al fondo de los cielos.
Posesión. Ya no oís la voz del cuco.
Qué ojo de dragón, qué fuego esférico,
qué tela roja, tafetán de brujas,
vela mis ojos? Llovió, y en la hierba
queda una huella. Mas he aquí que arde
nítido y muy lejano el bosque en torno,
un edificio, una pavesa sola,
una lanza hasta el último horizonte,
cual tirada a cordel. Nubes. El viento
no murmura palabras al oído
ni repite otra historia que ésta: ved
el castillo y los muros de la noche,
el zaguán, el reloj, péndulo insomne,
los cayados, las hachas, las segures,
ofertas a la sombra, todo cuanto
abandonan los muertos, el tapiz
dormido de hojas secas que pisamos
entrando a guarecernos. Pues llovía
—se quejaban las hojas—y el cristal
empañado mostró luego el incendio
como impostura. ¿Llegarán las lenguas
y la ira del fuego, quemarán
desde la base el muerto maderamen,
abrirán campo raso donde hubo
cerco de aire y silencio? No es inútil
hablar ahora del piano, los visillos,
las jarras de melaza, el bodegón,
los soldados de plomo entre serrín,

# ◆ *THE HARP IN THE CAVE*

The forest burned in silence.
The autumn clouds pursued
their chase in the depths of the skies.
Possession. You no longer hear the cuckoo's voice.
What dragon's eye, what spherical fire,
what red cloth or witches' silk
shades my eyes? It rained, and a print
is left on the grass. But see how the wood
burns bright and far, all around,
a building, a single ember,
a lance thrown hard and long,
towards the last horizon. Clouds. The wind
doesn't whisper words in your ear
nor repeat any other tale: see
the castle and the walls of the night,
the entrance, the clock, sleepless pendulum,
the shepherds' crooks, the hatchets, the sickles,
offerings to the shadow, all the things
the dead would leave behind, the sleeping tapestry
of dry leaves we step on
coming in for shelter. It was raining
—the leaves complained—and then
the blurred glass reflected the fire,
like an imposture. Will the tongues
and anger of the fire arrive, will they burn
the rotten timber to the ground,
and clear a space where once
a ring of air and silence stood? It isn't useless
to speak of the piano now, the curtains,
the jars of molasses, the wine cask,
the lead soldiers in the sawdust,

las llaves de la cómoda, tan grandes,
como en el tiempo antiguo. No es inútil.
Pero qué cielo éste del otoño.
La abubilla que habla a los espíritus,
la urraca, el búho, la corneja augur,
el gavilán, huyeron. Ni una sombra
se interpone entre el lento crepitar
y el cielo en agonía. Abrid un templo
para este misterio. Sangre cálida
dejó tu pecho suave entre mis manos,
amada mía: un goterón de púrpura
muy tembloroso y dulce. Como yesca
llameó la paloma sin quejarse.
La muerte va vestida de dorado,
dos serpientes por ojos. Qué silencio.
Tarda el fuego en llegar al pabellón
y hay que ir retirándose. Ni un beso
de despedida. Quedó sólo un guante
o un antifaz vacío. Cruces, cruces
para ahuyentar los lobos!
                              Un guerrero
trae la armadura agujereada a tiros.
En sus cuencas vacías hay abejas.
Lagartos en sus ingles. Las hormigas,
ah, las hormigas besan por su boca.
Espadas de la luz, rayos de luna
sobre mi frente pálida! Un instante
velando sorprendí a vuestro reflejo
la danza de Silvano. Ágiles pies,
muslos de plata piafante. El agua
lavó esta huella de metal fundido.
Y un resplandor se acerca. Así ha callado
el naranjo en la huerta, y el murmullo
de su brisa no envía el hondo mar.
Vivir es fácil. Qué invasión, de pronto,
qué caballos y aves. Tras las nubes
otras nubes acechan. Descargad

the bureau keys, so big,
like in the olden days. It isn't useless.
But what a sky, this autumn one.

The hoopoe that talks to the spirits,
the magpie, the owl, the ominous crow,
the sparrow hawk have fled. Not even a shadow steps
in between the slow crackle
and the agony of the sky. Build a temple
to this mystery. Your soft breast
has left warm blood between my hands,
my beloved: a very trembling, sweet
drop of purple. The dove,
like tinder, flamed up without a word.
Death is wearing a golden dress,
two serpents for eyes. Such silence.
The fire is slow in reaching the summer house
and you must begin your retreat. Not even a kiss
good-bye. Only a glove was left behind,
or an empty mask. Crosses, crosses
to frighten away the wolves!
                                    A warrior
has come with riddled armor.
Bees fill his empty sockets.
Lizards, his groin. The ants,
ah, the ants, kiss through his mouth.
Swords of light, rays of moon
on my pale brow! I watched for a moment
and caught the sylvan dance
in your reflection. Agile feet,
stamping silver thighs. The water
washed this print of melted ore.
A flash of light approaches. It's hushed the orange
in the grove, and the murmur of its breeze
doesn't carry forth the deepest sea.
It's easy to live. What a sudden rush
of horses and birds. Other clouds are lurking
behind the clouds. Let down

este fardo de lluvia. ¡Un solo golpe,
como talando un árbol de raíz!
Se agradece la lluvia desde el porche
cuando anochece y ya los fuegos fatuos
gimen y corretean tras las tapias,
como buscándonos. Recuerdo que encendías
un cigarrillo antes de irte. Luego
el rumor de tus pasos en la grava,
sobre las hojas secas. Nieve, nieve,
quema mi rostro, si es que has de venir!
Se agradece la lluvia en esta noche
del otoño tardío. Canta el cuco
entre las ramas verdes. Un incendio,
un resplandor el bosque nos reserva
a los que aún dormimos bajo alero
y tejas, guarecidos de la vida
por uralita o barro, como si
no estuvieran entrando ya los duendes
con un chirrido frágil
por esta chimenea enmohecida.

this burden of rain. Just one blow,
like a tree felled from the root!
We're glad for rain, from the porch,
when night falls and the ignis fatuus
have begun to rove and moan behind the walls,
searching us out. I remember you lighting
a cigarette before you'd go. Then
the sound of your steps in the gravel,
in the dead leaves. Snow, snow,
burn my face, if you must come!
We're glad for rain on this late
autumn night. The cuckoo's singing
in the green branches. The forest
saves a fire, a flash of light
for us who still sleep beneath tiles
and eaves, sheltered from life
by cement or clay, as if
the spirits hadn't begun to come in
with a fragile shriek
through the musty chimney.


*The Sea Is Burning* (1966)

# ◆ CELADAS

*Poetry is the subject of the poem.*

WALLACE STEVENS

## I

Dicen que Apollinaire escribía
reuniendo fragmentos de conversaciones
que oía en los cafés de Montmartre: perspectivas cubistas,
como los recortes de periódico de Juan Gris,
                  celadas
cuando el fondo es más nítido que la figura central,
en primer término, algo deformada, enteramente reducida a
    ángulos y espirales—los colores son más vivos en los
    ventanales del crepúsculo: un tintineo metálico
en la cabaña de la infancia—de eso hablaba Hölderlin
y eran salones: preceptor, damascos rojos, el espejo
    veneciano,
*Wozu Dichter in dürftiger Zeit,* y Goethe escribiría a Schiller
    que aquel muchacho amigo suyo,
aunque todavía algo tímido y con la natural falta de
    experiencia
(todo, en el tono de la carta, trasluce el benévolo desprecio
    del viejo ante la poesía de un joven: él ya había escrito
    versos y—le parecía—mucho más serenos, o mejores, o,
    cuando menos, con aquel clasicismo que garantizaría su
    perpetuidad),
porque el arte clásico se mantendrá siempre: Hölderlin, en
    sus últimos años, a su madre
le escribía muy respetuosamente, con las fórmulas
    aprendidas cuando niño,
y le pedía tan sólo unos calzoncillos, un par de calcetines
    mal cosidos, cosas pequeñas y obvias

# ◆ SNARES

*Poetry is the subject of the poem.*

WALLACE STEVENS

## I

They say that Apollinaire wrote
by putting together scraps of talk
he'd heard in Montmartre cafes: Cubist perspectives,
like Juan Gris's newspaper clippings,
         snares
where the background is clearer than the central figure,
and in the foreground, somewhat deformed, reduced to
   angles and spirals—there are livelier colors in the
   windows at twilight: a metallic clinking
in a childhood cottage—that's what Hölderlin talked about,
and they were rooms: a professor, red damasks, the Venetian
   mirror,
*Wozu Dichter in dürftiger Zeit,* and Goethe would write to
   Schiller that that young friend of his,
though still somewhat shy and, naturally, lacking
   experience . . .
(the whole tone of the letter reveals the old man's benevolent
   contempt for a younger man's poetry: he was a poet
   already and had written—he thought—more gracefully, or
   better, or at least in that classic style that would guarantee
   immortality),
since classic art always will prevail: Hölderlin, in his last
   years, was still writing his mother with the same respectful
   formulas learned as a child,
just asking for some undershorts, a pair of darned socks,
   little obvious things

como las de Rimbaud en Abisinia, o en el hospital
—*Que je suis donc devenu malheureux!*—
y los poetas acaban así: heridos, anulados, muertos-vivos, y
por eso los llamamos poetas.
¿Así? La crucifixión de algunos no es tal vez sino un signo,
y es el equilibrio de otros su grandeza y su muerte,
y la fosforescencia de Yeats (Bizancio, como un gong en el
crepúsculo) el precio que pagamos
por aquél cuyo nombre estaba escrito en el agua.
Porque algún precio debe pagarse, podéis estar seguros:
Eurídice yace aún muerta
sobre los conmutadores eléctricos y el azul de una sala tibia
como la caja de un piano de caoba.
El mundo de Orfeo es el de detrás de los espejos: la caída de
Orfeo,
como el retorno de Eurídice de los infiernos, las bicicletas,
los chicos que venían de jugar al tenis y mascaban
*chewing gum,*
rubias espaldas, cuerpos dorados—delicados—, las
muchachitas de calcetines colorados y ojos azules de
Adriático que bebían gin con naranja,
las que se bañaban desnudas en las novelas de Pavese y las
llamábamos chicas topolino,
(no sé si habéis conocido el topolino: era un coche de moda,
o frecuente, en los *happy forties*).
Pero ahora ya soy más viejo, aunque decir viejo sea
inexacto, pero el color del gin con naranja
où sont où sont the dreams that money can buy?


*II*


Este poema es
una sucesión de celadas: para el
lector y para el
corrector de pruebas

like Rimbaud's belongings in Abyssinia or in the hospital
  —*Que je suis donc devenu malheureux!*—
and poets always end up like that: hurt, canceled out, dead-
  in-life, and that's why we call them poets.
Always? Maybe some crucifixions are no more than signs,
  while other people's steadiness is their greatness and their
  death,
and the phosphorescence of Yeats (Byzantium, like a gong at
  dusk) the price we pay
for one whose name was writ in water.
Because something must be paid, you can be sure of that:
  Eurydice still lies dead
on the electric transformers and the blue of a warm room
  like the case of a mahogany piano.
Orpheus' world is the one behind the mirrors; Orpheus' fall,
like Eurydice's return from hell, the bicycles, the boys
  coming back from tennis, chomping on a piece of gum,
fair shoulders, golden bodies—delicate—the girls with red
  socks and blue Adriatic eyes, drinking gin and orange
  soda;
the ones in Pavese's novels, swimming in the nude, and we
  called them Topolino girls
(I don't know if you've ever heard of the Topolino: it was a
  stylish, well, popular car in the Happy Forties).
But I'm older now, although *old* isn't quite the word for it,
  but the gin-and-orange color
où sont où sont the dreams that the dollar can buy?


*II*


This poem is
a series of snares: for the
reader and for the
copy editor

y para
el editor de poesía.
                    Es decir,
que ni a mí me han dicho lo
que hay detrás de las celadas, porque
sería como decirme el dibujo
del tapiz, y esto
ya nos ha enseñado James que no
es posible.

and for
the publisher.
          In other words,
they haven't told me either
what's in the snares, because
that would be like telling me the picture
in the tapestry, and that
is exactly what James teaches us cannot
be done.

*Translated by John DuVal*

*The Mirrors* (1970)

# ◆ SEGUNDA VISIÓN DE MARZO

## I

La gente, en los barrios más oscuros,
con los faroles y el hollín—los muchachos que por la noche
    limpian chimeneas con manos tibias
y en los muros lacerados del hospicio dibujan inscripciones
    paleolíticas—un alce, una serpiente, la muerte de una
    yegua—
y bajo los faroles se besan y mueren a punta de navaja con
    *claqué*
y cuando la niebla se adensa empapa sus sombreros de
    copa—todo es aceite y humo en aquellas casas del puerto
donde van a parar los blancos escotes, la sangre de los bailes
    callejeros, las alcobas nupciales,
el acordeón de los *bals-musette,* ya un poco marchita la
    dueña, rubia muy mal teñida—pero los ojos azules son
    aún jóvenes—que fumaba *Gauloises,*
        y ahora, al caer la noche,
la llama de los *becs de gaz,*
como los labios de una mujer que besara mis párpados,
porque los ojos se cerraban para morir o para amar.

## II

Hace frío, en los barrios más oscuros, y la gente aún piensa
en la gorra de fieltro y el hule de una Browning en el bolsillo,
porque en las dos primeras esquinas no, pero en la tercera se
    quebrará de un puñetazo el vidrio
y las niñas que juegan en el callejón, como en un viejo film
    de Chaplin

# ◆ SECOND VISION IN MARCH

### I

The people, in the darkest boroughs of the city,
with lanterns and soot—the boys who clean the chimneys at
    night with warm hands
and sketch paleolithic inscriptions on the lacerated walls of
    the hospice—a moose, a snake, the death of a mare—
and beneath the lanterns, kiss and die at the point of a knife
    with *claqué*
and when the fog condenses, it wets their silk hats—it's all
    smoke and oil in the houses near the port
where the low-necked frocks end up, the blood from the
    street dances, the nuptial bedrooms,
the accordion of the *bals-musette,* its owner, a badly dyed
    blonde, withered a bit—but her blue eyes are still young—
    the one who smoked *Gauloises,* and now, when night
    falls,
the flame of the *becs de gaz,*
like the lips of a woman who'd kiss my lids,
since eyes were closed to die or to love.

### II

It's cold, in the darkest boroughs of the city, and the
people still think about the felt hat and the oilskin of
a Browning in a pocket, because, not on the first two
corners, but on the third, the window will break at the
    punch of a fist
and the girls playing in the alley, like in an old Chaplin
    movie

—rubias, un jersey de mortecino color, los ojos de perla
   marina—,
ahogadas con lazos y cintas y la oscuridad del Metro,
cuando la calle Aribau parecía salida de un noticiario de
   postguerra
(las muchachas enterradas en el Fossar de les Moreres, con
   consultorio sentimental y olor de almidón y de cocina—la
   radio, después de cenar, como una voz del país de los
   muertos),
alma, alma mía, ¿quién te llamaba a un estío de glicinas?

## III

Como los hombres que se cumplen en la acción, o en el
   deseo, o con un cuerpo tibio al fondo de un callejón,
al fondo de un diorama como los que había antes en los
   sótanos del monumento a Colón, representando el
   descubrimiento de América, al estilo de las composiciones
   de época del siglo pasado,
aunque se movía un poco el papel de las pitas, pintadas ante
   un dragón verde que enseñaba los colmillos en segundo
   término,
y todos en la piragua—los que surcamos las negras aguas del
   Leteo,
así el poema a un tiempo sufre la imperiosa necesidad de
   designar lo real
y no lo puede designar: le son precisas las paráfrasis
para aludir al tránsito de una nube en verano,
a la corola tibia que en los labios se deshace,
al sentimiento de nostalgia, al miedo, a la toma de contacto
   con las oscuridades de la memoria,
lo que hace y deshace el poema, la pérdida de contacto con
   la conciencia
que nos espera en un cóctel—y aquel hombre de smoking
es ya un hombre tan muerto como un actor de cine.
Así, pues, la palabra se convertirá en celada

—blond girls, sweaters of a deathly shade, eyes the color of
    sea-pearls—,
choked with bows and ribbons and the darkness of the
    subway,
when Calle Aribau looked like a street from a postwar
    newsreel
(the girls buried in the Fossar de les Moreres, with advice for
    the lovelorn and the smell of starch and kitchens—the
    radio, after super, like a voice from the land of the dead),
soul, my soul, who called you to a summer of wisteria?


## III

Like men who find fulfillment in action or desire, or with a
    warm body at the end of an alley,
at the back of a diorama like the ones in the cellars of the
    Columbus monument, representing the discovery of
    America, in the style of period compositions of the last
    century,
although the canvas moved a little, the one of the Bacchae
    painted before a green dragon in the middle ground,
    showing his fangs,
and everyone in the canoe—all of us cleaving through the
    black waters of the Lethe,
the poem suffers at once from the imperious need to
    designate reality
and it cannot: it needs paraphrases
to allude to the passing of a cloud in summer,
to the warm corolla that dissolves on lips,
to feelings of nostalgia, to fear, to coming in contact with the
    obscurities of memory,
what makes and unmakes the poem, losing touch with
    consciousness
which waits for us in a drink—and that man in tails
is already as dead as a movie star.
And so, words will become a snare

tan sólo en la medida en que lo queramos: ceniza o música,
es tal vez un esfuerzo de lucidez, y la simultaneidad de
   planos
corresponde en ella a la complejidad de una experiencia: es
   decir,
que no se podría explicar de ningún otro modo aquel
   momento entre dos estaciones, saliendo de Salzburgo,
con las luces y los rieles—ángulo rasante, un niño jugaba
   con la niebla—lúgubres, lúgubres,
y sólo un poema puede explicar por qué aquel hombre mal
   afeitado y ebrio tiene ojos de príncipe.
El hundimiento de un mundo: esto es la grandeza,
y tanto da que caiga una *vamp* con pieles de visón como un
   compañero de colegio del cual sólo recordamos las manos
   que temblaban bajo el pupitre una tarde de estío.

## IV

Nunca he vivido la distancia entre lo que queremos decir y
   lo que decimos realmente,
la imposibilidad de captar la tensión del lenguaje, de
   establecer un sistema de actos y palabras,
un cuerpo de relaciones entre el poema escrito y su lectura.
Quizá un discurso eliotiano en ocasiones, pienso
que este poema pone realmente en peligro
uno de los niveles de mi poesía: es decir, que el discurso
muestra aquí a un tiempo las dos caras del espejo.
   Lo cierro, y da la vuelta:
de noche, con luz, en la oscuridad dorada, en las calles o en
   la muerte,
como el rumor del bosque y los árboles que en él caen
   talados en silencio
—¿dónde, sino en mi corazón?

only in as much as we want them to: ashes or music,
perhaps it could be a striving for clarity, and the
simultaneity of planes corresponds to the complexity of
the experience: in other words, there's no other way to
explain that moment between two stations, leaving Salsburg,
with the lights and tracks—and right beside, a little boy was
    playing with the mist—mournful, mournful,
and only a poem can explain why that badly shaven,
    inebriated man has the eyes of a prince.
A world caving in: this is greatness,
and it doesn't matter who falls, a vamp draped in mink or a
    school chum whose hands we remember, nothing more,
    trembling beneath his desk one summer afternoon.


### IV

I've never experienced the distance between what we mean
    and what we really say,
the impossibility of capturing the tension of language, of
    setting up a system of words and deeds,
a body of relationships between the written poem and its
    reading.
At times perhaps an Eliotian essay: I think
this poem really endangers
one of the levels of my poetry: in other words, the essay
shows here both faces of the mirror at once.
    I close it up, and it turns around:
at night, with lights, in the golden darkness, on the street or
    in death,
like the sound of the forest and trees that are felled there in
    silence
—where, but in my heart?


*The Mirrors* (1970)

# ◆ A Poem from APARICIONES

Había un buey oscuro en el camino
y me paré para escuchar. Las letras
luminosas y líquidas de la gasolinera
y el rastrillo de plata de un grillo. Había aceite
vertiéndose en la noche.
　　　　　Allí no estaba el mundo,
y estaba más que nunca: era un cuerno de caza
que sonaba a lo lejos.
　　　　　　　　　Yo conozco la noche
sintética, prisión de plásticos que hierven,
resplandor sofocante y helado que respira
para ahogarme el pecho. Ante todo, el silencio
se definirá en términos de noche natural:
la noche de la tierra antes del hombre, noche
del hombre antes del ser. Respirar, muy despacio,
como no respirando, como si respirar
fuese vivir del todo, como si nuestra vida
no nos bastase para sentir que respiramos.
¿Sentir cómo respira el mundo? Sí, alguna vez,
en un cerro, la idea de un dominio, quizá
la de una paz que conciliase el mundo
con su apariencia. Desde dentro a fuera,
un camino que une y separa: los términos
de lo que es y lo que vemos. Late
como una maquinaria lejana de la noche:
nunca cesa. Cerrarse al sonido, saltar
fuera de este único rumor,
como presa desnuda en los colmillos
de la noche que vive y que jadea.
No engullido: a distancia, suspendido, sin centro,
saltar fuera del centro, ver respirar el mundo.

# ◆ APPARITIONS, *Poem III*

There was a dark ox in the road
and I stopped to listen. The liquid,
luminous letters of the gas station
and the silvery rake of a cricket. There was oil
spilling out in the night.
          The world wasn't there,
and was present more than ever: it was a hunting horn
sounding in the distance.
                 I'm familiar with synthetic
night, a prison of boiling plastics,
a smothering, frozen splendor that chokes me
with its breath. And midst it all, the silence
will define itself in terms of natural night:
the night of earth before man, the night
of man before being. To breathe, very slowly,
like not breathing, as if breathing
were drawing life from the whole, as if our lives
weren't enough to let us know we breathe.
Sense how the world breathes? Yes, once,
on a hill, the idea of a dominion, perhaps
the idea of a peace that might conciliate the world
with its appearance. From the inside out,
a road that joins and separates: the limits
of what exists and what we see. It beats
like some distant mechanism of the night:
it never stops. Close yourself to the sound, jump
away from this singular noise
like a naked prey in the fangs
of living, panting night.
Not swallowed up: far off, dangling, without a core,
jump away from the core, see the world breathe.

*Apparitions* (1983)

# MANUEL VÁZQUEZ MONTALBÁN

*Barcelona, 1939*

# MANUEL
# VÁZQUEZ
# MONTALBÁN

Manuel Vázquez Montalbán was born in July, 1939, a few months after the Civil War. The suffering of his family, particularly his father, in prison when his son was born, deeply affected his early years. His childhood and adolescence were spent in a working-class neighborhood of Barcelona, and before manhood he experienced little more than what that zone had to offer—his home, school, local movie theater, and youth club. The harsh realities of his life there contributed a great deal to his poetic development. His sense of marginality and his response to the urban experience would shape his writing, even into middle age. As a high school student, he planned for a career in automobile mechanics; but, encouraged by a history teacher who recognized his potential as a writer, he decided to attend college. His enrollment at the University of Barcelona led to his first extensive encounter with the middle class and the language of bourgeois culture, which, with its generalizations and conceptual abstractions, seemed almost indecipherable for a youth of his background.

His entrance into the university, coinciding with the mid-fifties student movement, also put him in contact with political minorities, illegal in Spain at that time. He read Sartre, Lefevbre, and leftist aestheticians like Trotsky and Della Volpe, who reinforced his inclinations toward vanguard art. Just before completing his degree, in 1962, he was arrested during a student demonstration and imprisoned for a year and a half. He wrote incessantly during that time and finished most of the poems of *Una educación sentimental* (An Education on Feelings) 1967, and *Movimientos sin éxito* (Unsuccessful Movements) 1969; as well as a novel, a book of essays on journalism, and several translations of the Italian authors, Pratolini, Maestronardi and Volpini. One of the ironies of the Franco dictatorship must be that such a prolific and dissident writing career should begin in a fascist prison.

Among the poets included in this anthology, Vázquez Montalbán is the only one who, by reason of social and political affinities, might be linked with the social realist aesthetic of many other postwar poets. Nonetheless, his literary personality, both as novelist and poet, is so much the reverse of the social realist. His feelings of solidarity with the economically and socially oppressed never developed into a testimonial posture in his poetry but nurtured instead a talent for objective observation, a keen ability to perceive patterns of social and historical development, and a gift for finding pathos and humor in many philosophies and patterns of comportment. Unlike the "social" poets, he believes that poetry is ineffective as a political weapon and that if poetry is to make a statement, it must do so indirectly, through irony, its most corrosive implement. Also setting him at variance with the social realists, he never concerns himself precisely with the communication of a message but approaches each poetic venture as a search for artistic solutions.

His first book, *Una educación sentimental*, recaptures memories from childhood and adolescence; yet the first poem in the collection, "Nothing Was Left of April . . . ," reaches beyond the poet's birth to a moment in history prior to the Civil War. It creates a before-and-after vision of his birthplace, Barcelona, a tranquil place and then a postwar wasteland, like Eliot's Waste Land, alluded to in the title. This poem contains a key emotional moment in Vázquez Montalbán's early verse, since the reactions of the child persona, who sees destruction but fails to grasp the reality of the larger conflict, establish the mental posture of other voices in the collection. Like actors in a dramatic irony, they live out their lives in the shadow of a vague, nameless event, which, although definitive to their state of mind, reveals itself essentially in the humiliation and guilt that it inflicts on its victims.

As the persona grows older, his thoughts turn to love; and in one of the early love poems, "Yramín the Gothic," the poet puts to use a technique learned from Eliot, that of drawing parallels between the small dramas of contemporary life and mythic or legendary events. Using this technique, he composes poems which illustrate the interrelatedness of past and present, fiction and reality. In "Yramín . . ." fantasy enters the poem through a legend of the poet's own creation. Like the medieval Provençal poets, he creates a secret name for his lover ("Yramín") based on an anagram of her real name Myrian and an epithet ("la gótica") suggestive of Barcelona's Gothic Quarter. The name and place provide an idyllic setting for the monologue of the decidedly modern protagonist, who fluctuates between fantasy and the reality of his daily routine, but ultimately discovers that to live in a fantasy world is to learn that one must abandon it. When his "damsel" hops into a taxi, the disillusioned lover leaves his never-never land, which perhaps never existed at all, and returns to a mundane life.

Unlike most of the poems in this first book, the poem "Gauguin" is not autobiographical, and possibly for this reason was included in the final section of the book, entitled "Liquidación de restos de serie" (Clearance Sale). This poem reveals Vázquez Montalbán's special talent as a painter of lyrical portraits. In a short space, he is able to create an image of a life, one which is not totally known until the last word is read. An artisan at synchronizing a variety of materials, he combines the lyric with the prosaic, the sounds of poetry with the humdrum of common discourse, and many voices with that of the main speaker—a voice that balances praise with irony and fact with emotion. Later on, he would employ these skills in a much longer and complex poem, *Coplas a la muerte de mi tía Daniela* (Couplets on the Death of My Aunt Daniela) 1973, which begins as a lyrical portrait and develops into a commentary on contemporary life.

In "Sentimental Mail. Response to Enide," from his second volume, *Movimientos sin éxito,* Vázquez Montalbán draws his characters from Chretien de Troyes' *Erec et Enide,* which, in his words, "crystallizes the myth of love which must be rejuvenated each day" (my 1976 interview).[1] In combining medieval and modern details which simultaneously describe the mythical Erec and his modern counterpart, the poet produces an interesting two-directional effect. While the myth, as Eliot said, gives "a shape and a significance" to the contemporary event (426), the contemporary elements, which evoke a kind of insignificance or triviality associated with modern technological advancement, render the romantic fantasy ironic and divest the mythical characters of their aura. Readers of the poem, encouraged to reconsider their notions of both fantasy and contemporary experience, may wonder if the medieval lovers are essentially different from the modern ones.

*Coplas a la muerte de mi tía Daniela* challenges readers to make similar comparisons. The poet, searching for a structure which might order contemporary European history and at the same time give meaning to one meager existence, turns to a monument of late medieval Spanish poetry, Jorge Manrique's *Coplas a la muerte del Maestre don Rodrigo, su padre* (Couplets on the Death of Master Rodrigo, His Father). At first Vázquez Montalbán seems to be parodying Manrique's elegy: the implied comparison of a simple washerwoman and a hallowed nobleman would certainly suggest this interpretation. But the poem goes beyond a mere parody to explore the meaning of contemporary existence. Using irony, the poet exposes the corrosive effects of technology and utilitarian standards, and arrives at conclusions similar to Manrique's: in spite of the fugacity of human existence, a life, however small, is worthy of praise.

For certain, Vázquez Montalbán enjoys tampering with myths, but it would be misleading to call him a "demythologizer." To read him thoroughly, we must notice that, at his hand, myths and heroes seem to lose little more than their fantasy. Upon entering the contemporary sphere of the poem, the characters become strangely human, and we get to know them—perhaps come to like them—more than we did before. *A la sombra de las muchachas sin flor* (In the Shadow of the Flowerless Girls) 1973, however, is myth tampering of another kind. Here the poet rips away at the idealized, unattainable woman, who was never his and whom he hopes to find someday dead "on a big, stuffed mattress / the cornhusks / sticking out through the unstitched places of the world" (37–8).[2] This appears to be his mental position in many poems from this collection. In other poems, like "Moral Reflections on the Anatomy," his position is entirely different.

When women are attainable, they become "fruit for parched lips / for hands / with no other world to be clutched to the soul" (27).[3] The last of the amorous-erotic poems, "Epilogue for Drowned Men," suggests neither of these positions. It allows two voices to speak, a sea horse and a man, and also allows two positions to be expressed. While the sea horse rambles on about elementary logic and living in the present, the man drowns in the memory of an erotic experience, oblivious to the reasoning of the sea horse.

In *Praga* (*Prague*) 1982, his last and perhaps most difficult collection of verse, he explores a repertory of associations which make Prague—the repeatedly besieged city, the city of Mozart and Kafka—into a symbol of alienation and provisional identity. Confronted with the stark reality of destruction and the fallibility of all dogmas, the poet voices his most negative thoughts on modern civilization. Whether speaking of Communists (Part I) or Catholics (Part III), he is utterly cynical. Though at first glance these poems seem quite different from Vázquez Montalbán's earlier verse—perhaps because of the shift away from Barcelona to a foreign setting, on closer analysis numerous similarities are revealed. There is both stylistic and thematic continuity between this volume and his first collections, and many of its poems, like the erotic love poems or lyrical portraits, harken back to compositions from *Una educación sentimental, Movimientos sin éxito,* and *A la sombra de las muchachas sin flor.* The historical undertaking of *Praga,* as it attempts to piece together private lives and public events, recalls *Coplas a la muerte de mi tía Daniela.* A parallel is also evident between the psychological make-up of the persona of the earlier verse and Kafka, an important voice in the last volume. Each is involved in a struggle for identity which occurs within a context of conflict, loss, and cultural alienation. In this regard, Barcelona and Prague play historically similar roles, and the voice which says, "I didn't choose to be born among you / in the city of your terrors" (27),[4] might be either Kafka speaking to the citizens of Prague or Vázquez Montalbán speaking to the people of the Catalan capital.

Perhaps the readjustment of voice, distanced from the poet's own milieu, is the primary change in this volume which otherwise sums up the major themes, ranging from the erotic to the political, treated in his first four volumes. By choosing Prague as a setting, he places the marginality theme in another context. But the voice that speaks from the sidelines and the inimitable irony that divests people and institutions of their sanctity, these elements are the same.

# POEMS

# ◆ NADA QUEDÓ DE ABRIL . . .

Era distinto abril, entonces
había alegría, y rastro de mejillones
en la escollera, canciones
a la orilla del crepúsculo, pretendientes
vanamente apostados en las esquinas,
tras las persianas verdes remendadas,
tras los geranios alimentados con moñigos
de percherones lentos, espiábamos
la variación anormal de la chaqueta a cuadros
Príncipe de Gales
     los pañuelos de rayón
blancos como paloma en el pecho, zapatos
de charol como bombillas negras, silbidos
largos, insinuantes, cuchillos de gasa sobre
la piel, si mamá se entera o vecinas
al acecho de honras ajenas
        y más tarde
los gitanos del Bar Moderno, tamboril
de silla, canción de salmuera o la voz
del musclaire
     *arri Joan que l'arròs*
*s'està covant*
       felices tiempos de reyes asequibles,
Alfonso XIII borbónico y flemático pasaba
como pasan los reyes, con majestad,
          por el ensanche
cuando íbamos a entregar los largos
calzoncillos de felpa a Inogar Hermanos
         Confecciones

# ◆ NOTHING WAS LEFT OF APRIL . . .

April was different, then
there was joy, and mussel shells
along the shore, songs
on the shore of twilight, suitors
idly stationed on corners
behind the green mended shades
behind the geraniums fertilized with the litter
of slow draft horses, we spied on
the abnormal variations of the plaid
Prince of Wales jacket
                        the rayon handkerchiefs
white like a dove on their chests, patent leather
shoes like black lightbulbs, long
insinuating whistles, gauze knives
against the skin, if Mother finds out or the neighbors
lying in wait for other people's reputations
                                        and later
the gypsies at the Modern Bar, a chair
for a drum, a saltwater song or the voice
of the mussel vendor
                        *arri Joan que l'arròs*
*s'està covant* *
                        happy times of accessible kings
Alfonso the Thirteenth phlegmatic and Bourbon would pass
as kings do, with majesty,
                                through the outskirts
when we would turn in the long
muslin underwear at Inogar Brothers
                                        Dry Goods

* hurry John the rice / is burning.

MANUEL VÁZQUEZ MONTALBÁN   73

grises atardeceres de máquina Sigma,
Wertheim, Singer
      Singer, me inclino por la Singer
                              cansa
menos los riñones, pero una tarde de abril
                    entonces
en el rompeolas, compensaba trescientos
sesenta y cuatro días de viajes ensoñados,

haciendo calados, dobladillos, festones es posible
llegar hasta Suecia, John Gilbert y Greta Garbo
se aman tiernamente, respetuosamente, imposiblemente

                    la tabla de encarar
puede ser una vasta llanura de amores gauchos
y la curva para el vientre una ensenada
donde atraquen veleros olorosos en betel y especias
con marinos dispuestos a la muerte
                    por Jean Harlow

                    pero a veces
pasaban multitudes vocingleras por la calle
                      *Visca*
*Macià qu'és català, mori Cambó qu'és un cabró*
y papá habló con un marino de bigotes amarillos
en un mercante
                sobre la hamaca la luna de Benicasim
era la misma que la de Mazarrón, llegamos
a un puerto entre rocas doradas, parientes,
fotografías animadas, tardes por la Glorieta
en sillones de mimbre, pay-pays de cartón blanco
con anuncios de Linimento Sloan

              nada quedó del puerto,
grúas retorcidas, patrulleros hundidos, serones
cargados de alcaparras y girasoles, cascotes

gray afternoons of Sigma sewing machines,
Wertheim, Singer
      Singer, I prefer Singer
               it doesn't tire
my back as much, but one afternoon in April
             then
at the breakwater would make up for three hundred
sixty-four days of imagined journeys

making lace edging, hems it's possible
to get to Sweden, John Gilbert and Greta Garbo
love each other tenderly, respectfully, impossibly

              the facing board
might be a vast plain of Gaucho romances
and the curve for the abdomen a bay
where aromatic vessels might dock loaded with mint and
  spices
with sailors prepared to die
        for Jean Harlow

           but sometimes
noisy multitudes would pass along the street
           *Visca*
*Macià qu'és català, mori Cambó qu'és un cabró* †
and Papa talked with a yellow-whiskered sailor
on a merchant ship
      from the hammock the moon of Benicasim
was the same as the one at Mazarrón, we reached
a port through golden rocks, relatives,
animated photographs, afternoons in the park
on bamboo chairs, pay-pays of white cardboard
with advertisements of Sloan Liniment

         nothing was left of the port,
twisted cranes, sunken patrol boats, baskets
loaded with caper-bushes and sunflowers, rubble

†Long live / Macià who's Catalan, down with Cambó who's a son of a bitch.

MANUEL VÁZQUEZ MONTALBÁN  75

de bombas misteriosamente humanizadas, se oían
caer después, ya de vuelta a la ciudad, como
una noche impuesta que se impone gritando

                                        murieron
pretendientes y nadie descendió a la calle
al paso de los percherones
                los geranios
se agostaron en cenizas amarillas
                        luego
volvieron otras tardes de abril, no aquéllas
                                muertas
muertas ya para siempre

                los gitanos perdieron duende, no
cantaban, tosían de noche bajo el relente, cuando
cosíamos tristes arreglos de vestidos viejos
para mutilados cuerpos de postguerra
                                incivil

inmutables, más allá de esta ventana, de esta
persiana, de estas macetas vacías como planetas
deshabitados, los palos grises para tender
la ropa, azoteas de arenisca y ladrillos desportillados,
negras chimeneas rotas
            y amarillos jaramagos sobre tejados en erosión.

from mysteriously humanized bombs, you would hear them
dropping later on, on the way back to the city, like
a night inflicted, inflicted screaming

                              they died
suitors still and no one went out on the street
when the draft horses passed by
                        the geraniums
dried up into yellow ashes
                then
other April afternoons returned, not those
                                  dead
dead forever

        the gypsies lost their magic, they didn't
sing, they coughed at night under the mist, while
we sewed sad patches on old clothes
for mutilated bodies of an uncivil war

unchanged, beyond this window, beyond
these shades, beyond these pots empty like uninhabited
planets, the gray poles for hanging out clothes,
sandstone tiles and broken bricks,
black broken chimneys
              and yellow dandelions on eroding rooftops.

*An Education on Feelings* (1967)

# ◆ YRAMÍN, LA GÓTICA

Las hilachas de lluvia y aquel
quejido duro de la piedra
en la Plaza del Rey teníamos tiempo
de olvidar las ocho y cuarto
y presagiarnos mutuas lentejuelas
de futuro brillante
                    qué tristes
decidimos ser tristes y sarcásticos
y cómo la alegría fue sencilla
hasta las ocho y cuatro

                    un café
quemado como un recuerdo inútil
tal vez otro café y la conversación,
cultos los silencios, teníamos
aún más imágenes que palabras
                              gratuita
la alegría porque a las ocho y un cuarto
movedizo la patria y potestad
protegía tu sexo del relente nocturno

todavía creíamos un poco en las cosas
lineales, y era lineal el tiempo, los ojos
nos unían por líneas castas y parpadeos
sedosos, de satén poco gastado
                              pero a las ocho
y cuarto volvíamos al mundo de ellos
y las islas del Nunca Jamás se oscurecían
hasta mañana

# ◆ YRAMIN, THE GOTHIC

Streams of rain and that
harsh moaning of the stone
in the Plaza del Rey we had time
to forget eight fifteen
and to foresee mutual sequins
of a bright future
                    how sad
we decided to be sad and sarcastic
and since joy was simple
until eight fifteen

                    a burned coffee
like a useless memory
perhaps another coffee and conversation,
the silences, cultured, we had
even more images than words
                              gratuitous
joy because at eight and a variable fifteen
the homeland and the potentate
protected your sexuality from the night fog

we still believed a little in linear
things, and time was linear, our eyes
held us together with chaste lines
and battings of the eye, silky, of little worn satin
                                        but at eight
fifteen we went back to their world
and Never-Never Land grew dark
till the morrow

y fue que de repente
te encaramaste a un taxi y al día siguiente
supe que las islas jamás han existido
                              y que el tiempo
suele iniciarse sobre las ocho y cuarto.

and it happened that suddenly
you got into a taxi and the following day
I knew that the Land never has existed
and that time
usually begins about eight fifteen.

*An Education on Feelings* (1967)

## ◆ GAUGUIN

Periodista
su padre
escribió artículos notables
la libertad—decía—
es una dignidad popular
y sin embargo
murió rumbo a Lima
donde Pablo cumpliría once años
una mañana—a las once y cuarto—
de junio
    mil ochocientos cincuenta y nueve

marinero
después en un buque de carga
descubrió los olores
el salazón las brumas de Bretaña
siempre amaría
las bajamares infinitas
              entonces
cuando parece que la huida
del mar lleva consigo
nuestros males oscuros
          la ira abstracta

pero todavía
sirvió en las filas de aquel ejército
que no supo cortar
el avance prusiano
        —Bismark comentaba
que el soldado francés era cobarde
y tan ligero como su ropa interior—

# ◆ GAUGUIN

His journalist
father
wrote notable articles
liberty—he'd say—
is a dignity of the people
and nevertheless
he died on the way to Lima
where Paul would turn eleven
one morning—at eleven fifteen—
in June
            eighteen fifty-nine

later on
a sailor
on a cargo ship
he discovered the perfumes
the seasoning the mist of Brittany
he would always love
the infinite low tides
                    and later
when it seems that escaping
to the sea carries along
our dark maladies
                    abstract anger

but still
he served in the ranks of the army
that couldn't block
the Prussian advance
                    —Bismarck observed
that the French soldier was a coward
and as flimsy as his underwear—

nada experto
en socialismo utópico
recordaría tal vez a su padre
                    cuando
el ejército de Thiers fusilaba
a los redactores del Journal Official

no muy al día
nunca supo que Marx
                    —judío alemán—
hubiera escrito «... esos mártires
han penetrado en el gran corazón
de la clase obrera»
                    inútil aclararlo:
eran los días de la Comune

                    atraído
por los café concierto
la sensación caldosa del buen mundo
Gauguin quiso tener faltriquera
y el suelo firme
para una sombra por todos respetada

pintaba los domingos paisajes inseguros
                              —el impresionismo
ya no era una pirueta y las duquesas
de la tercera república tenían su Monet—
durante la semana
era un probo agente bursátil
muy alabado por M. Arosa
coleccionista de Pissarro y gran connaisseur

en la agencia de cambio Bertin
le describen como un joven severo
de impecable levita y bigote
algo provocativo pero correcto
hasta el bostezo
                    incluso algo lento

                              not expert
in utopian socialism
he may have remembered his father
                              while
Thiers' army was shooting
the editors of the Official Journal

not very up-to-date
he never knew that Marx
                    —a German Jew—
had written ". . . those martyrs
have penetrated the great heart
of the working class"
                    useless to make it clear:
those were the days of the Commune


                              attracted
to cafés concerts
the luscious feel of the good life
Gauguin wanted a full purse
and firm ground
for a shadow respected by them all

on Sundays he painted uncertain landscapes
                              —impressionism
was no longer a pirouette and the duchesses
of the third republic had their Monet—
during the week
he was an upright broker
quite praised by M. Arosa
a Pissarro collector and great connoisseur

at the Bertin exchange
they describe him as a severe young man
of impeccable dress and moustache
somewhat provocative but correct
to the yawn
              even a little slow

en las respuestas como los pajes
o los gobernadores del Banco de Francia

casado en Copenhague,
tuvo hijos y siguió pintando los domingos
en la Bolsa, aseguraban,
cada vez estaba más distante
y los clientes se complacían en la tristeza
por un joven antaño tan prometedor

nadie sabe cómo consiguiera romper el abrazo
mañanero de un cuerpo blando
y propicio aunque fétido el aliento
amanecido recuerde la elemental biología
que respalda al amor

                   ni cómo consiguiera
prescindir de las raíces
                 —sus hijos
le tenían por un padre severo
pero humano, en suma un padre
de manual pedagógico finisecular—

viajero en Panamá
París, Bruselas o Bretaña
sus pinceles fueron debilitando
el cosquilleo de cualquier remordimiento
su derecho a la locura
fue ratificado por Vincent Van Gogh
aunque en Arles todo demuestra que durmieron
en habitaciones separadas
                en el café Voltaire
intentó comprender los versos que leía Mallarmé
Stephan insistía
            c'etait le jour beni
de ton premier baiser
                pero Gauguin
permanecía silencioso

in answering like the pages
or governors of the Bank of France

married in Copenhagen
he had children and kept on painting on Sundays
at the Stock Exchange, they were sure,
he was more and more distant
and the clients took delight in their sadness
for such a formerly promising young man

no one knows how he managed to break
the morning embrace of a body, soft
and willing, though the breath is foul
at dawn it may rouse the biological urge
that sustains love

                    nor how he managed
to give up his roots
                    —his children
thought him a stern father
but human, all in all a textbook
fin de siècle father—

a traveler in Panama
Paris, Brussels or Brittany
his brushes gradually softened
the twinge of any remorse
his right to madness
was ratified by Vincent Van Gogh
although in Arles everything proves they slept
in separate rooms
                    in the café Voltaire
he tried to understand the verses read by Mallarmé
Stéphane insisted
                    c'etait le jour beni
de ton premier baiser
                    but Gauguin
kept silent

                              hubiera querido
pintar aquellos versos mas no tenían
color ni tan siquiera una emoción humana

no bastaba
la huida de la Bolsa del desayuno
normativo
las mismas palabras se repiten
siempre si los cuerpos no cambian

en Tahití
las autoridades miran con recelo
al extranjero blanco amante de canacas
no entendieron que intentaba objetivar
lo subjetivo
            y que la animalidad
tierna de las canacas era casi el fin
del viaje vital de Paul Gauguin

desterrado a las Marquesas
conoció la cárcel por sospechoso
de no infundir sospechas
                            en París
se le tenía por un snob empedernido
sólo algunas nativas conocían su impotencia
pasajera
            y que l'or de ses corps
                        era un pretexto
para olvidar las negras sillerías de las lonjas
el cucú de un comedor de Copenhague
un viaje a Lima con una madre triste
las pedantes charlas del café Voltaire
                        y sobre todo
los incomprensibles versos de Stephan Mallarmé.

he wanted
to paint those verses but they had no
color nor even human feeling

the flight from the Stock Exchange from a breakfast
of the ordinary kind
was not enough
the same words keep repeating
forever if the bodies do not change

in Tahiti
the authorities suspiciously eyed
the white foreigner a lover of yellow-skinned women
they didn't understand that he was trying to objectify
the subjective
            and that the tender
animality of those women was almost the end
of life's journey for Paul Gauguin

exiled to the Marquesas
he got to know the jail on suspicion
of not creating suspicion
            in Paris
they took him for a hard-hearted snob
only some native women knew of his passing
impotence
            and that l'or de ses corps
                        was a pretext
for forgetting the black benches of the salerooms
the cuckoo of a dining room in Copenhagen
a trip to Lima with his sad mother
the pedantic conversations in the café Voltaire
                        and above all
the incomprehensible verses of Stéphane Mallarmé.


*An Education on Feelings* (1967)

## ◆ CORREO SENTIMENTAL.
## RESPUESTA A ENIDE

Hijita,
      triste riesgo el ser más que nadie
incluso para el amor, no es cierto
que aquellos caminos de Bretaña, aquellas
calles de Bretaña, aquellos subterráneos
de Bretaña fueran suyos
               en las tardes
en que más tiritaban los semáforos
                   y las gentes
descendían hacia el puerto
              —se esperaba,
la llegada de un buque de nombre extranjero
que nunca atracó en el puerto al anochecer

pero ustedes volvieron una y otra vez, quizá
no por repetidas las palabras se invaliden
signifique siempre siempre
              siempre nunca nunca
nunca y aunque tarde, más tarde siempre
de la hora fronteriza del regreso a casa
lleguen
        iluminados mástiles del buque fantasma
y los amantes no esperen el ciclo de los meses
para ser tres, ni los padres expulsen
de lechos conyugales a parejas, exiladas
del crepúsculo
           triste hambre, dulce hambre
                    pero ahora, Enide
las imágenes rotas deben convencerla
de que nunca llegará a algún lugar

My dearest child,
                    a sad risk being better than everyone else
even in matters of love, it's not true
that those roads of Brittany, those
streets of Brittany, those subways
of Brittany were yours
                    in the evening
when the stoplights shuttered most
                              and people
went down to the harbor
                    —they'd be waiting,
for a boat with a foreign name
and it never docked in the harbor at dusk

but you two returned again and again, perhaps
it's not through repetition that words lose their meaning
perhaps always always means
                              always never never
never and although late, always later
than the last hour for returning home
they might come in
                    shining masts of the phantom boat
and perhaps lovers do not await the monthly cycle
to become three, nor do fathers throw
couples from conjugal beds, exiles
at twilight
                    sad hunger, sweet hunger
                                        but now, Enide
the broken images should convince you
that you'll never reach anywhere

del que no quiera regresar
                    ¿los recuerdos?
abstractas tumbas de ladrillo, de hiedra
artificial, biblioteca grave y roja chimenea
a fuego lento
                y tú y yo, tú y yo
                        pero en el puerto
nunca llegará—nunca llegaría—el buque
de nombre extranjero y los desencantos conducen
a la evidencia de que ningún buque llega para nadie

en cuanto a Erec
lleva la armadura remendada, traduce
libros sobre ardillas del inglés, vive
de mala manera en una playa llena
                        de pintores abstractos.

you won't wish to return from
                            memories?
abstract tombs of brick with artificial
ivy, somber library and red hearth
slowly burning
                and you and I, you and I
                                    but at the harbor
it will never come in—never would—the boat
with a foreign name and disenchantments lead
to the conclusion that no boat ever comes in for anyone

as for Erec
he's wearing patched armor, translates
books on squirrels from English, leads
a frightful life on a beach full
                            of abstract artists.


*Unsuccessful Movements* (1969)

◆ *Selections from COPLAS*
*A LA MUERTE*
*DE MI TÍA DANIELA*


No siempre
los recuerdos miman
juventudes
ni aleccionan
como diccionarios caros
o cartas publicables

inútiles
vicios sentimentales
amanecen
anochecen
con nosotros
         lujuria
de sensaciones
extras vinos de festival
de máscaras

inútiles
permanecieron
         ahora
resucitan
al pie de un son
un lugar
una fotografía
en ocasiones
pretexto pudo ser
un jirón
de media
o cicatrices

◆ *From* COUPLETS
ON THE DEATH
OF MY AUNT DANIELA

Memories
do not coddle
childhood
always
nor instruct
like costly dictionaries
or publishable letters

useless
sentimental vices
they grow light
grow dark
with us
          lust
of emotions
extra-fine wines
for masquerades

useless
they remained
                    now
they come to life
sparked by a sound
a place
a photograph
the pretext could be
at times
a scrap
of stocking
or scars

de remiendos
como una piel
fallida

y si la muerte
toma parte
pertenece al fantasma
oscura
reaccionaria
escasamente planificable
entonces
el recuerdo abisma
suspende
convenciones estables
enfría un café
un adiós
una caricia
un minuto de porvenir
tan cuestionable

porque los muertos
presiden las constelaciones
pero disienten
de los proyectos espaciales
de las carreras
premiadas con limonadas
artificiales
vastas ladys
compotas prefabricadas
ya tarde

plácido el sauce
                llorón
de mala madre

estúpidamente lógica
sin designio
                llega

from patches
like faltered
skin

and if death
takes part
it belongs to the dark
reactionary
phantom
barely projectable
then
memory plunges
suspends
stable accords
makes a coffee cold
a good-bye
a caress
a minute of future
so questionable

because the dead
command the constellations
but disapprove
of projects in space
of races
rewarded with instant
lemonade
vast ladies
processed mixtures
too late

placidly the weeping
               willow
son of a bitch

stupidly logical
without design
          arrives

sin guadaña
secreta
sorbe alientos
hiela miradas
deja
estadísticas optimistas
tantos
por ciento de superaciones
edades medias
mejoradas
con respecto
al Asia del Gran Kan

las ciudades arrullan
consuelos eléctricos
horarios
destrozones de piedad
sepultan
muertos
antaño sin sepultura
y la concreta
necesidad de la necesidad
justifica
el miedo a los olvidos


por todo ello memoria traigo
para mi tía Daniela
Monterde Viader
o Viadell
              nunca lo supo
hija de Sinarcas
ilustre fregona
mala lengua
cigarra
en el pobre hormiguero
proletario
de la España de charanga

without a secret
scythe
sucks up breaths
stops glances cold
leaves
optimistic statistics
such and such
a percent of survivals
age expectancies
improvements
with regard
to the Asia of the Great Khan

the cities coo
electric comfort
schedules
destroyers of pity
entomb
the dead
formerly unentombed
and the concrete
necessity of necessity
justifies
the fear of unmindfulness


for all this I bring memory
to my Aunt Daniela
Monterde Viader
or Viadell
            she never knew
daughter of Sinarcas
illustrious maid
grasshopper
in the poor proletarian
anthill
of the Spain of marches

y pandereta
devota de Belmonte
y de María

nunca supo
que mereció ser triste
el balance de su vida
ignorante
de la sabiduría que rebela
desespera
estetiza los cansancios
puso su corazón
al ritmo del instinto
y su cerebro
al de un cuplé
insustancial

no hablan de ella
las crónicas humanas
las lápidas
las estelas
las columnas
ni las nostalgias
de los hijos que no tuvo
los amores
que no le sobrevivieron
ni las olas
fugitivas como agua
en sucia
sumisión de vertedero

ningún caminante
de regreso
hubiera visto su nombre
luminoso
en las cúspides de la ciudad
de acero

and tambourines
devotee of Belmonte
and Mary

she never knew
the balance of her life
should be sad
ignorant
of the wisdom that rebels
despairs
finds beauty
in weariness
she set her heart
to the rhythm of instinct
and her brain
to the meaningless song
of a cabaret

human chronicles
tablets
steles
columns
do not speak of her
nor nostalgias
of children she never had
the loves
that didn't survive her
nor the fugitive
waves like water
in dirty
submission to the drain

no traveler
homeward bound
would see her name
in lights
on the cusps of the city
of steel

en los cruces
de caminos
                ni siquiera
en la memoria
de un papel a soplos
de un viento amarillo

sólo
mi voluntad
de constructor de siglos
ahoga en las palabras
la zozobra
de un remordimiento
la angustia
de un dolor concreto
irrepetible
acusación de un dedo
puro muerto

at a cross
in the road
        not even
in the memory
of a piece of paper tossed
by a yellow wind

only
my will
as a builder of centuries
chokes
with words
the anxiety
of remorse
the anguish
of a certain sorrow     .
unrepeatable
accusation of a finger
purely dead


*Couplets on the Death of*
*My Aunt Daniela* (1973)

# ◆ REFLEXIÓN MORAL SOBRE LA ANATOMÍA

Hay mujeres que hacen daño
en el pecho del que muere
                    al contemplar
la contención exacta de su carne
                          la refrigeración
blanda de sus cabellos limpios
y el pretexto caedizo de sus ropas

                              otras
tienen los ojos tristes pero hermosos
o un bello lomo para un torpe frente
                              o dos piernas
sin cansancio muscular columnas
                          de seguro cielo

otras sólo tienen
dos senos a punto de abrirse por su peso
de fruta para labios agostados
                          para manos
sin otro mundo que llevarse al alma

                              y en ocasiones
sólo un seno es hermoso sólo un hombro
sólo un vencimiento de la piel
                          sólo los labios

pero siempre hay un hombre enamorado de tanto o de tan
    poco
enamorado fugaz o consecuente ama

# ◆ MORAL REFLECTIONS
## ON THE ANATOMY

There are women who bring pain
to the heart of the one who dies
                              contemplating
the exact confinement of their flesh
                              the soft
coolness of their clean hair
and the slippery pretext of their clothes


                              others
have sad eyes but lovely
a beautiful side for a dull front
                              or two legs
with untiring muscles columns
                              of unfailing glory


others only have
two breasts about to burst from their weight
fruit for parched lips
                    for hands
with no other world to be clutched to the soul


                              and sometimes
only one breast is lovely only one shoulder
only one victory of the skin
                              only the lips


but there's always a man in love with so much or so little
fleeting lover or reliable he loves

las pequeñas patrias de una noche
                              sin clarines
frente a unos párpados cerrados murmullos
fracasadas sintaxis

                    respetad las plantas
y los cuerpos donde el deseo se descansa
del infinito miedo a todos los olvidos.

the small homelands of a night
                              without trumpets
before closed lids murmurs
defeated syntax

                    please respect the plants
and the bodies where desire rests
from the infinite fear of being forgotten.

*In the Shadow of the Flowerless Girls* (1973)

# ◆ PONME LA MANO AQUÍ

*y yo sin saber qué hacer*
*de aquél olor a mujer*
*a mango y a caña nueva . . .*

CHAVELA VARGAS


Cuando te encuentre
en el trastero del mundo
                    Chavela
me mostraré indiscreto
                    quisiera
saber qué fue de tu Macorina
si supiste qué hacer
                de aquel olor a mujer
a mango y a caña nueva

                    te perdono
las mujeres que me hayas quitado
a cambio de que me cantes
                    cuerpos prohibidos
calientes como danzones color
canela humedecida por los deseos

                        cuando te encuentre
con los pies en un barreño de lágrimas
los ojos caídos de perro perdido
el cabello sucio por cenizas y viajes
                        Chavela
quisiera que cantaras la muerte de Macorina
sobre un colchón tripudo
                    las hojas de maíz
salientes por los descosidos del mundo

# ♦ TOUCH ME HERE

*and how could I tell*
*what to make of the smell*
*of women, mangos and new cane*

CHAVELA VARGAS

When I find you
in the backroom of the world
                              Chavela
I won't be discreet
                    I'll want
to know what became of your Macorina
if you found out what to do
                              with that smell of women
of mangos and new cane

                              I'll forgive you
for the women you've taken away
if you'll give me in return a song of
                              forbidden bodies
hot like those slow rhythms the color
of cinnamon damp with desire

                              when I find you
with your feet in a tub of tears
your eyes drooping like a lost dog
your hair dirty with ashes and journeys
                              Chavela
I'll ask you to sing me the song of Macorina's death
on a big, stuffed mattress
                    the cornhusks
sticking out through the unstitched places of the world

MANUEL VÁZQUEZ MONTALBÁN    109

la vieja Macorina seguramente mal amada
en los años en que no fue tuya
                    ni mía
sino un cuerpo progresivamente absurdo
abandonado por las guitarras y las quejas.

old Macorina ill-loved for certain
during the years when she wasn't yours
                                    or mine
but only a body growing progressively absurd
abandoned by guitars and laments.


*In the Shadow of the Flowerless Girls* (1973)

# ◆ EPÍLOGO PARA AHOGADOS

Pero—me dijo el hipocarpo—
sus deseos no sobrevivirán
y ni la más estricta sabiduría
conseguirá restituirle un instante perdido

era espumosa la noche
sobre las terrazas ruidosas
bogaba el batelero del Amazonas
en el centro de mi deseo
tus senos cerraban tus ojos
y entre tu breve mimbre
mis dedos buscaban el húmedo gemido

pero—añadió el hipocarpo—
usted puede aferrarse al hábito
de lo que no ha hecho, incluso
al hemisferio de los números imaginarios

qué levemente corrías oscura
breve frío de desnudo al aire
olía a pólvora nocturna y blanca
y bastaba avanzar para tenerte
suspensa de lo que no haría
al cerrarte el cuerpo exacto

pero—se impacientó el hipocarpo—
usted prescinde de la lógica elemental
la que mata lo vivo y hace nacer
esperanzas a base de olvidos y distancias.

# ◆ EPILOGUE FOR DROWNED MEN

But—the sea horse said—
your desires won't live forever
and not even the strictest wisdom
can retrieve a lost moment

the night was foamy
above the noisy terraces
the boatman of the Amazon was paddling
in the middle of my desire
your breasts your eyes were closing
and my fingers round your tiny twig
searched for the moist groan

but—the sea horse added—
you can stick to the habit
of what you haven't done, even
to the hemisphere of imaginary numbers

how nimbly you ran dark
brief cold of a naked body in the air
a smell of powder from the rockets, nocturnal and white
and just moving towards you I'd have you
in suspense of what I wouldn't do
when I closed your body just right

but—spoke the sea horse impatiently—
you're omitting elementary logic
that kills what's alive and gives birth
to hopes founded on distance and things long forgot.

*In the Shadow of the Flowerless Girls* (1973)

## ◆ Poems from PRAGA

### From Part I

Os reconozco
en vuestro retrato predilecto
músculos tensos
la historia es horizonte
armas o herramientas
          ultimátums
de decisivas huelgas fracasadas
o asaltos al Palacio de Invierno
                cada verano

he respetado vuestros cuentos
para dormir de noche amanecer
               de día
les di camino fueron mi sombra

mas no os fiéis de mi entusiasmo
demasiado distante para creer
todos los días a todas horas
              todos juntos

demasiado necio para huir
de toda tierra todo abrazo
           todo tiempo
condenado a vivir lejos morir cerca
nocturno de día diurno de noche
animal o flor equivocados
             quiero
cuando debiera odiar
         vivo
cuando hasta los jaramagos tiemblan de presentimiento

## From Part I

I can pick you all out
in your favorite portrait
muscles tense
history's an horizon
weapons and tools
        ultimatums
of conclusive strikes that fail
or attacks on the Winter Palace
          every summer

I've respected your stories
to sleep at night to rise
        by day
I gave way to them they were my shadow

but don't trust my enthusiasm
too distant to believe in
every day every hour
        all of you at once

too stupid to run away
from every place every embrace
        all time
condemned to live far away to die nearby
nocturnal with the day diurnal at night
mistaken animal or flower
        I love
when it's time to hate
        I live
when even the dandelions tremble with dread

MANUEL VÁZQUEZ MONTALBÁN   115

*From Part II*

Nacer en Praga en 1883
significaba ser súbdito
del imperio austro-húngaro
Francisco José despilfarrador de Historia
Sissí madre de hijos asesinables
finalmente dinamitada
      por un anarquista consecuente

Kafka por parte de padre
Amschel por parte de madre
comerciantes que jamás leyeron a Kafka
niño con ganglios y terrores precoces
Praga fue primero escuela primaria
sillón patriarcal para padres
           sin remordimientos

abogado y fugazmente socialista
protestó en mil novecientos nueve
por el asesinato de Ferrer Guardia
conmemoró el cuarenta aniversario de La Comuna
amó a las mujeres para cartearlas
y Milena Josenska le tradujo al checo
en un vano intento de repatriarle
tras descubrirle cierta poquedad sexual

                en alemán
Kafka describió el terror de ser hijo y ciudadano
o a acaso padre y estado fueran
           —al decir de Benjamin—
las dos arqueologías de su sabiduría:
rumor de cosas verdaderas y locura

               Praga
era castillo sótano de justicia
gran muralla china al final
del vano esfuerzo por salir de uno mismo
a través de estancias achicadoras
            de toda estatura

## From Part II

Being born in Prague in 1883
meant being a subject
of the Austro-Hungarian empire
Franz Josef History's squanderer
Sissi mother of assassinatable children
blown up at last
                    by a responsible anarchist

Kafka on his father's side
Amschel on his mother's
businessmen that never read Kafka
a child with precocious glands and fears
Prague was foremost a grammar school
a patriarchal chair for parents
                              without remorse

a lawyer and fleeting socialist
he protested in nineteen hundred and nine
the assassination of Ferrer Guardia
celebrated the fortieth anniversary of the Commune
loved women so he could write them
and Milena Josenska translated him to Czech
a vain attempt to return him to his country
once she knew of his sexual smallness


                              in German
Kafka described the horror of being a son and a citizen
or perhaps father and state were
                              —in Benjamin's words—
the two archeologies of his wisdom:
a rumor of true things and madness


                              Prague
it was a castle a cellar of justice
great wall of China at the end
of the futile effort to get out of oneself
through rooms that diminish
                              any stature

calles del castillo calles de Praga
                              laberinto
para el judío que escribe en alemán y asume
insuficientemente la tradición del Talmud
                    la esperanza de Sión

olor de padre mujer ciudad ilimitable
                              Praga
capital de República en mil novecientos veintidós
fugaz soberana entre dos ocupaciones
Kafka siguió escribiendo en alemán
entre recelos checos y desdenes judíos
en esta época se le ve joven vampiro
en una calle plaza foto sin salida
realizada por un fotógrafo kafkiano
                    avant la lettre

tuberculosis mudez sanatorio Wiener Wald
muerte en Kierlig no lejos de Viena
enterrado en Praga junto a un padre metafísico
y a una madre insuficientemente literaria
profeta de Hitler y del vietnamita cósmico
sus hermanas fueron gaseadas a oscuras
y sus obras quemadas por sospechosas
                    de decadencia e irrealidad

aunque Benjamin le supone sentido del humor
nada indica que su última obra
—Josefina la cantante o el pueblo de los ratones—
fuera un desplante a la ciudad versátil
contemplada desde un punto de vista tuberculoso
ciudad del terror entre las avenidas
lívidos árboles del otoño

                    aunque todo es posible
en un hombre que pidió la destrucción de sus obras
al único judío que no iba a hacerlo

castle streets streets of Prague
               labyrinths
for the Jew who writes in German and inadequately
assumes the Talmud tradition
               the hope of Zion

the smell of a father woman unlimitable city
               Prague
capital of the Republic in nineteen twenty-two
fleeing sovereign between two occupations
Kafka continued writing in German
between Czech misgivings and Jewish scorn
he seemed a young vampire then
in some street square a snapshot that didn't come out
made by a Kafkan photographer
               avant la lettre

tuberculosis muteness sanatorium Wiener Wald
death in Kierling not far from Vienna
buried in Prague next to his metaphysical father
and not so literary mother
prophet of Hitler and the cosmic Vietnamese
his sisters were gassed in the dark
and his works burned suspected
               of decadence and unreality

although Benjamin assumes he had a sense of humor
nothing suggests that his last work
—Josephine the singer or the mouse folk—
may be a mistaken move to the versatile city
contemplated from a tubercular perspective:
city of terror on the avenues
livid autumnal trees

               although anything is possible
in a man who left the destruction of his works
to the only Jew who wouldn't do it

## From Part III

Bien está
que necesitéis la muerte
para creer en la vida
o que pidáis perdón
cuando no podáis exigirlo
                    ya no tenéis remedio

pero es excesivo
que os perpetuéis desnudos
para morir vestidos
por el orgullo de que alguien os entierre
y ensaye su propia muerte
                    en la vuestra

no tengáis hijos

dejad que las tortugas recuperen la tierra
y ni siquiera memoricen
la sopa de tortuga
                o la victoria sobre Aquiles
manipulada por los filósofos

no condenéis a muerte
al inocente que descubrirá ya muerto
no haber nacido inmortal
ni invisible en los espejos
                    del espacio y el tiempo

a lo sumo
extingámonos sin dolor
reservando la tierra para las penúltimas parejas

y la última que se suicide
para evitar la conspiración de las serpientes

## From Part III

It's fine
that you need death
to believe in life
or that you ask forgiveness
when you can't demand it
                        you're past help

but it's a bit extreme
your staying nude
to then die dressed
out of pride in someone burying you
and rehearsing his own death
                        though yours

don't have children

let the turtles inherit the earth
and don't even learn
turtle soup by heart
                   nor the victory over Achilles
manipulated by philosophers

don't condemn the innocent one to death
who'll discover once dead
that he wasn't born immortal
nor invisible in the mirrors
                      of space and time

at most
let's reach extinction without pain
saving the earth for the next to the last couples

and let the last one commit suicide
thus escaping the snakes' conspiracy

*Prague* (1983)

# GUILLERMO CARNERO

*Valencia, 1947*

# GUILLERMO
# CARNERO

Guillermo Carnero, born in Valencia in 1947, was a published poet before the age of twenty. There is much autobiography concealed in his verse: the first years of education at a French school in Valencia, the marginality of a free-spirited youth coming of age in the stifling, authoritarian society of postwar Spain, avid reading in art history, literary theory, and philosophy, travel to France and Italy (though his first knowledge of the latter came through Ruskin and other writers), and difficulties of an amorous nature which sent him fleeing to England.

Carnero's poetry does not focus on these specific experiences, however. As indicated by the title of his collected poems, *Ensayo de una teoría de la visión*, 1966–1977 (Testing a Theory of Vision) 1979, the focus is primarily theoretical and visual. One reading of the word *ensayo* is "essay" in the sense of "treatise"; another meaning is "experiment" or "try out." The latter, which suggests the testing of an idea more than the positing of knowledge, is more relevant to Carnero's undertaking, since he concerns himself with trying out a series of beliefs and not with speaking definitively about them. The topics which he tests include reality, memory, language, and poetry.

Carnero, as a poet, seeks a formula for expressing what he sees, thinks, and feels. Frustrated by the inadequacies of his medium, he fluctuates between two styles of discourse: one which proceeds directly, feigning rationality, and another which is essentially descriptive and symbolic. He often changes from one style to the other in the same poem, combining argument or commentary with lyrical descriptive passages. The contrast is rather striking. It would seem that when the poet opens the door to reason, a dazzling array of objects—monuments of the past or relics of a deserted carnival—enters the poem. When reasoned discourse occurs, it easily becomes a victim of its own linguistic ambiguities, puzzling even the most attentive reader. The poem's imagery, similarly imprecise—or at least the poet would have us think so—fades like the picture in an outworn tapestry. The brillance of the experience, diminished by deficient memory and obscure words, leaves behind nothing more than "a pitiful / chromatic subtlety" ("una pobre / sutileza cromática" [203]).[1]

With images drawn from life and art and concepts selected from readings and his own philosophical musings, the poet engages in a constant play of fragmentation and irony. He seems to hold the objects he describes in doubtful esteem. The exquisite or magnificent ones tumble down with the myths they pertain to—the ancient world in the poem "Paestum," the neo-classical period in "Les Charmes de la vie" and "Setting Sail for Cythera," and bourgeois society in "Perpetual Motion." Some of his other objects are more literally hollow, deformed, or strangely sad, like a stuffed bird, a collection of old toys, or the handful of small items drawn from a poor man's pocket.

Whereas the irony in Carnero's images is often the irony of decadence or separation, the irony of his concepts is that of "razón racionalista" ("rationalistic reasoning"), a term which Carlos Bousoño employs in his prologue to Carnero's collected works (16). According to Bousoño, many of the writers of Carnero's generation have rejected the kind of reasoning which, removed from experience, relies on generalization and abstraction, and makes utility its first concern. The rejection of "rationalistic reasoning" produces philosophical rumblings at many levels, and in Carnero's case, it affects most visibly his views on language. Since language depends heavily, perhaps entirely, on abstraction and generalization, he deems it incapable of presenting any given reality. This disenchantment with language creates a major irony for the poet and his readers as well. Readers of this poetry find themselves in the awkward position of responding to a medium which belies its own capacity to communicate. If they accept Carnero's position, that poetry is an exercise in futility, what must they believe about their own participation in the poem? On the other hand, if they interpret Carnero's position as a mere challenge to reexamine their own assumptions about language, they may conclude, with Bousoño, that poetry, though incapable of presenting reality, acts as a valuable "cifra" (cipher [25]) of a mental image.

Carnero does not offer an immediate solution to this dilemma. He chooses rather to sustain an ironic posture throughout many poems in *Dibujo de la muerte*. His title implies that poetry is a "sketch of death," "sketch" suggesting the frailty or incompleteness of any image, and "death," the lifelessness of communicated experience. In "Avila," the first poem in the collection, the poet, describing a tomb, contrasts the intricate spectacle of art with the difficult task of preserving knowledge: "But I know there's nothing of you in your books, / in your words, nothing can be known, nothing / can you show" (78).[2] Several poems from this collection and later volumes reveal more aspects of Carnero's disenchantment: "Perpetual Motion" suggests a parallel between the "modest masquerade" ("modesto baile de disfraces" [84]) of the bourgeoisie and an abandoned carnival. The poem ends with a rhetorical question, a common device in Carnero's poetry: "tell me if it was worth the trouble to have lived for this: / for turning to the creaking of the tarry boards, / for turning and turning until death" (85).[3] In "Les Charmes de la vie," using imagery inspired by Watteau's *fête galante* of the same title, the poet indicates a different strategy. Why not follow the example of Anacreon: "Why not be calm if everything is lost?" ("¿Cómo no serenarse, si todo está perdido?" [96]). "Setting Sail for Cythera," also inspired by a Watteau painting, carries disillusionment into the sphere of human relationships. By means of an ironic epigraph, "Sicut dii eritis"—the serpent's promise to Adam and Eve that the apple will make them god-like—the poem draws an analogy between the serpent's deceit and love's transformational power. Still another myth, the enlightenment of the gods, is rendered ironic in "Paestum" (from *Variaciones y figuras sobre un tema de La Bruyère*), where the poet depicts the issue of intelligence as a "progeny of lucid ghosts" ("su progenie de fantasmas lúcidos" [160]).

In the triad of poems which ends his collected works—this last section is also entitled *Ensayo de una teoría de la visión*—the poet synthesizes earlier statements on reality, memory, language, and poetry. In "Discourse on Voluntary Servitude"—a possible reference to the writer's servitude to words—he takes up the argument begun in "Objective Chance," an earlier poetic "essay" on the arbitrariness of memory. The writer ponders first how a poem comes into being, inspired perhaps by something as insignificant as a "smell of tar or damp earth" ("un olor de alquitrán o de tierra mojada" [199]), and then how the poet haphazardly gathers up the pieces of an experience, giving them "theatrical reality" ("veracidad escénica" [199]). Throughout the creative process, perhaps chance is the only determining factor, deciding both the subject of the poem and its realization.

The second poem, "Le grand jeu," treats the poet's inability to fix the color and emotion of an experience. Carnero suggests that a different approach may be valid for writing poetry. Reverse the process, he says: "not from the emotion to the poem but vice versa" ("no de la emoción al poema / sino al contrario" [204]). Since neither image nor emotion can be taken directly from reality and put into the poem, the text must be viewed as an act of creation, and if not a resurrection, at least the source of new images and emotions. The last poem, "Ostend," constitutes a tacit acceptance of the poet's dilemma. In full awareness of his limitations, he obediently undertakes his work as a manipulator of words. He concludes that poets and readers alike can best equip themselves for poetry by accepting from the outset that "the word is the only thing at the journey's end" ("no hay más que la palabra / al final del viaje" [207]). Nevertheless, poetry, he believes, is worth our time, since words, though "empty and fleshed like the staves and axles of planetary models" ("vacía y descarnada como duelas y ejes de los modelos astronómicos" [207]), can make a "perfect architecture" ("una perfecta arquitectura" [207]) of experience. The last lines of "Ostend" slide neatly into the beginning of Carnero's volume, the title of the first collection, *Dibujo de la muerte:*

> Composing a discourse [sketch]
> is no longer a sign of life, but the best proof
> of its end [death].
> Discourse isn't born
> in the void,
> but, yes, in our awareness of the void.
> (208)[4]

When his experiment with vision ends, when the poet has carefully studied the characteristics of his own visual mechanism, he reaches a mental position which is not at all pessimistic. He accepts the arbitrariness of the sign and its isolation from reality, both emotion and object; and yet, apparently undisturbed by the fallibility of his medium, he invites readers, all those who are lovers of words, to content themselves with simply *viewing* the spectacle of the poem. "Ne voise au bal qui n'aimera la danse" (75).[5]

# POEMS

En Avila la piedra tiene cincelados pequeños corazones de
 nácar
y pájaros de ojos vacíos, como si hubiera sido el hierro
 martilleado por Fancelli
buril de pluma, y no corre por sus heridas ni ha corrido
 nunca la sangre,
lo mismo que de los cuellos tronchados sólo brota el mismo
mármol que se entrelaza al borde de los dedos
en un contenido despliegue de pétalos y ramas,
en delgados cráneos casi trasparentes en la penumbra de las
 bóvedas
que conservan la ligera sombra azul de los ojos yertos en las
 raíces de la lluvia,
la morbidez, las redondas mejillas de los niños nacidos al
 mármol para la muerte,
los senos vagamente estériles de las Parcas diluidas en rígidos
 ramos de volutas y frutos,
el doloroso latir de las irisadas tibias sobre los cojincillos de
 mármol, ondulados
como para ofrecer un reposo caliente y amortiguar la
 delgadez helada
de esa mano de ámbar que acaricia con el pausado ritmo de
 la lluvia
la cabeza de un perro también muerto en la piedra,
muerto en la piedra junto a unos dedos y un cuerpo
 demasiado hermoso para haber vivido,
muerto en la piedra mientras se escucha brotar hacia la
 tumba
toda una inmensa vegetación de alas.
Luego, por la ciudad, tiene la noche
un lejano horizonte de olivos y acaso alguna ermita

# ◆ AVILA

In Avila minute nacre hearts and empty-eyed birds are
 chiseled into stone
as if the iron Fancelli hammered were a burin of feathers,
and blood does not and never has flowed from their wounds
just as from the truncated neck there rushes forth only the
 same marble that laces the tips of the fingers
in a restrained unfolding of petals and branches,
in thin, almost transparent skulls in the half light of vaults
that conserve the light blue shadow of eyes fixed in the roots
 of the rain
the morbidity, the round cheeks of children born to marble
 for death,
the vaguely sterile breasts of the Fates indistinct among the
 fruits and rigid scrollwork branches,
the mournful palpitation of the rainbowed tibias on little
 marble cushions, undulating
as if to offer a warm repose and to muffle the frozen thinness
of that amber hand, caressing to the unhurried rhythm of the
 rain
the head of a dog, also dead in the stone,
dead in the stone next to fingers and a body too beautiful to
 have lived,
dead in the stone while toward the tomb can be heard
 rushing forth
a whole undergrowth of wings.
Then, throughout the city, the night holds
a distant horizon of olive trees and perhaps a hermitage

entre las llamas color de cardo que suben hasta las figurillas
　　de bronce de las fuentes,
los jirones de almenas lamiendo entre la noche
el torturado brazo de las norias,
los jirones de almenas ardiendo como un turbio
arroyo, entre el helado crepitar de las fuentes,
entre el resbaladizo gotear, en el aire
de la estepa, del sordo sonido de los siglos.

A pesar de la noche, es imposible
reconstruir su muerte.
Ir ensamblando antiguos inciensos y sudarios,
medallones, y viene hasta mí el golpeteo
de un caballo en los lisos espejos de la noche,
es imposible, nadie sabrá, ni esas raíces
ni esas pequeñas uvas de humedad y salitre
ni ese tenue azabache como el salto de un pájaro
que al trasluz se desliza en los atardeceres
al fondo de la carne de los ángeles muertos en el mármol.

Hay algún bar abierto en donde suena un disco.
Es tan vasto tu reino que no puedo llenarte,
pero yo sé que nada hay de ti entre tus libros,
en tus palabras, nada puede saberse, nada
puedes mostrar.
También tú has recibido la oscura herencia de un inmenso
　　dominio inaccesible
que no tiene ni principio ni fin ni esperanza en el tiempo.
Pero hoy algo renace en las pequeñas flores de óxido de las
　　órbitas vacías,
levanta por entre los hacinamientos de escorias ecos y
　　presencias de pájaros,
transcurre con un ligero temblor de alas por los delgados
　　caminos de la sangre, despierta
amortiguadas voces al fondo de los cuerpos; inicia
los ahogados latidos de los fríos corazones de hierro.

between the thistle-colored flames rising toward the bronze
   figurines of the fountains,
the pennants licking the night from the battlements,
the tortured arms of water wheels,
from the battlements the pennants burning like a turbid
stream in the frozen crackling of the fountains,
in the slippery dripping in the air
of the plains, of the deaf drumming of the centuries.

Even though it is night, it is impossible
to reconstruct their death.
To go about gathering ancient incenses and shrouds,
medallions, and the gallop
of a horse on the smooth mirrors of the night reaches me,
it is impossible, no one will know, not even those roots
or those moist little nitrate grapes
or those jet trinkets tenuous as the hop of a bird
slipping away into the filtered light of evenings
into the heart of the flesh of angels dead in the marble.

Somewhere there's a bar with a jukebox playing.
Your kingdom is so vast I cannot fill you.
But I know there's nothing of you in your books,
in your words, nothing can be known, nothing
can you show.
You have also received the dark inheritance of a huge
   inaccessible dominion
with neither beginning nor end nor hope in time.
But today something is being reborn in the little rust flowers
   of the empty sockets,
which from among the heaps of rubble raises echoes and
   presences of birds,
flits with a light trembling of wings through the paths of
   blood, awakens
calls muffled deep in the bodies, starts
smothered heartbeats in the cold iron.

Por eso, entre el inmenso latido de la noche,
elevado entre un rumor de vides húmedas, es triste
no tener ni siquiera un puñado de palabras, un débil
recuerdo tibio, para aquí, en la noche,
imaginar que algún día podremos
inventarnos, que al fin hemos vivido.

Therefore, in the great throb of the night,
raised up in a rumor of wet grapevines, it is sad to have
not even a handful of words, a faint
memory so that here in the night
we can imagine someday being able
to invent ourselves and at last to have lived

*Translated by John DuVal*


*Sketch of Death* (1967)

# ◆ EL MOVIMIENTO CONTINUO

*. . . pronto envejeceremos: moriremos*
*antes de conocer la libertad.*

ROBERT HERRICK

Las personas comme il faut, honestos padres de familia y
    demás gente de principios
(fotógrafos profesionales, profesores de baile y otros agentes
    de la autoridad)
tenían desde antiguo organizado su modesto baile de
    disfraces.
Y lo peor no fueron los ridículos gestos de las matronas,
    torpes animales domésticos,
ni el parloteo de los intrascendentes animalillos partidarios
    del orden y la compostura,
sino el distinguir, debajo de la pacotilla y de las flores de
    plástico,
su buena fe de gansos soñolientos.

En las afueras, después de haber dejado atrás las últimas
    viviendas del suburbio
—«glorria y prrez sempiterrnas», como dijo el santo varón,
    arrastrando las erres—,
encontramos en el crepúsculo, sin demasiado esfuerzo,
el modesto tinglado de una feria vacía:
ositos mecánicos, muñecas caucásicas para neuróticos
—cada una contiene otra igual, más pequeña,
    indefinidamente—,
espejos cóncavos, convexos y cóncavoconvexos,
barracas donde un coro de malolientes atletas vociferaba el
    canto del cisne,
antifaces de muselina, ciudadanos disfrazados de asnos de
    Persia,
asnos de Persia disfrazados de ciudadanos,
una completa historia del traje,
y muchas otras cosas, como por ejemplo, varitas mágicas,

# ◆ PERPETUAL MOTION

*We shall grow old apace, and die*
*Before we know our liberty.*

ROBERT HERRICK


Proper people, upright fathers of families and all other
   persons of principle
(professional photographers, dancing masters and other
   agents of authority)
long ago organized their modest masquerade.
And the worst part was not the ridiculous nods and becks of
   the matrons, dull domestic animals,
nor the chitchat of shallow little creatures dedicated to order
   and deportment,
but the perception, beneath the claptrap and the plastic
   flowers,
of their sleepy gooselike good intentions.

On the outskirts, after having left the last dwellings of the
   city behind
—"eterrrnal honorrr and glorrry," as the pious old man
   said, rolling his *r*'s
in the twilight, without much effort, we found
the modest platform of an abandoned carnival:
mechanical teddy bears, Russian dolls for neurotics
—each contains another like it, but smaller, *ad finitum*—,
mirrors, concave, convex and concave-convex,
barracks where a chorus of smelly athletes bellowed the song
   of the swan,
muslin masks, citizens dressed up as Persian donkeys,
Persian donkeys dressed up as citizens
a definitive history of fashion
and many other items, such as magic wands,

GUILLERMO CARNERO   139

insectos de cartón-piedra,
una colección bastante amplia de cremas para payasos,
la botella de porcelana rosada donde el prestidigitador
guardaba su elixir
para aparecer vivaracho y chispeante en público,
tres o cuatro chaquetas reversibles, las memorias de Frégoli
y un manual de Etiqueta Cortesana, con anotaciones
manuscritas
de Oscar Wilde, y alguna raspadura de Baudelaire.
Alguien descubrió que el tiovivo podía seguir girando,
mientras un organillo
oculto bajo las tablas martilleaba una mutilada *Chanson de
Cour*
reconocible, con un poco de buena voluntad.
Vosotros, mientras en la noche resuena
la rutilante música de circo,
decidme si merecía la pena haber vivido para esto,
para seguir girando en el suave chirrido de las tablas
alquitranadas,
para seguir girando hasta la muerte.

cardboard insects,
a fairly complete collection of clown make-up,
the rose-colored porcelain bottle where the magician kept his
    elixir
to make him look lively and spritely in public,
three or four reversible jackets, the memoirs of Fregoli
and a manual of Courtly Etiquette, with hand-written
    annotations
by Oscar Wilde and some erasures by Baudelaire.
Somebody discovered that the merry-go-round could keep
    on turning while the barrel organ
hidden under the boards hammered out a mutilated
    *Chanson de Cour,*
recognizable, with a bit of good will.
All of you, while the night reechoes
with the glittering circus music,
tell me if it was worth the trouble to have lived for this:
for turning to the creaking of the tarry boards,
for turning and turning until death.

*Translated by John DuVal*


*Sketch of Death* (1967)

## ◆ LES CHARMES DE LA VIE

*Watteau*

Que no turben las aves el crepúsculo.
Va a comenzar el vals. Que todo quede
en tinieblas. Que las sedas oculten
las abiertas ventanas, y que alguien desenlace
los gruesos terciopelos. Nada debe
amenazar el flujo de la música:
ninguna arista o mármol o pájaro dormido.
Que nada permanezca. Sólo el aire
ilumine las fuentes ocultas de la noche,
difunda en las estancias un resbalar de remos
en los estanques, prenda el roce de las hojas
que desordena el viento entre las alamedas,
apague los destellos sobre los ventanales,
que las cortinas pongan su caliente aleteo
sobre cada cristal, para que los espejos
no descubran de dónde brotan los surtidores,
para que no resbalen hacia las balaustradas
las serpientes del agua, para que en la penumbra
los colores del mármol y de los terciopelos
desprendan un ingrávido gorgotear de luces,
y así, por un redondo laberinto de cauces
poco a poco la música, brotando de la oscura
trasparencia del aire, irrumpa desde cada
cristal amortajado, desde cada moldura,
libere sobre el musgo las voces de la noche
para que en el silencio girando las corrientes
heladas, ni los dedos ni la curva del torso
de la estatua disientan de la inmóvil presencia

# ◆ LES CHARMES DE LA VIE

*Watteau*

Don't let the birds disturb the twilight.
The waltz is about to begin. Let everything
stay dark. The silks should block
the open windows, and someone, undo
the velvet drapes. Nothing
should interfere with the flow of the music:
no angle, no marble, no sleeping bird.
Nothing should remain. Only the air
should light up the hidden fountains of the night,
and throughout the rooms, let there be a slapping of oars
on ponds. Seize the rustling of leaves
disturbed by the wind in the poplar groves,
put out the sparkle in the window panes,
let the curtains settle with a warm flutter
against each glass, so that the mirrors
can't find out where the fountains sprout from,
so that the water serpents won't slide to the balustrades,
so that in the shadows
the colors of marble and velvet
will let loose a weightless gurgle of lights,
so that at last, through a rounded labyrinth of river beds,
little by little, the music, sprouting from the dark
transparency of air, may break in from each
shrouded pane and from each molding;
let loose the voices of the night over the moss,
so that in the silence, while the icy currents
whirl, neither the fingers nor the arched torso

de los vasos que oprimen en las encrucijadas
un puñado de inertes raíces sumergidas.

Anacreonte supo renunciar a casi todos los mitos de su
    tiempo:
patria, fama, triunfo, dignidad de soldado,
respeto hacia los muertos y amistad con los dioses.
¿Cómo no serenarse, si todo está perdido?
Las montañas azules, a lo lejos, van siendo lamidas por la
    sombra.
Dibuja los contornos de las torres lejanas
la palidez helada de un viento submarino,
iluminando el brillo de los ojos, nítidos y cercanos
pero imposibles, como el rastro de umbría verdura que
    sugiere
el escondido cauce de un río subterráneo.
Que resuene el laúd, porque las voces
quebrarían el aire de la tarde.
Que los dedos desaten, entre los encajes,
el unánime llanto de las cosas,
pero que nadie intente otra vez pulsar las raíces de la vida.
Con el sol poniente van a lanzar sus últimos destellos, sobre
    las hojas amarillas,
las irisaciones de la música,
y los dioses silvestres convocan al silencio en la espesura.
Que nadie intente descubrir los sones
originarios.

        La noche desciende
sobre las tazas de las fuentes mudas, como las hojas muertas,
y oprime con mano tibia los atributos de la música:
latón pulido de las cornamusas,
resonancias que cierran su corola junto a los bucráneos
festoneados de racimos y cintas.
Ahora resbala por las escalinatas
la múltiple aureola de las luces

of the statue will clash with the still presence
of the vases in the crossroads that press
a submerged fistful of inert roots.

Anacreon was able to renounce almost all the myths of his
     time:
country, glory, success, a soldier's dignity,
respect for the dead and fellowship with the gods.
Why not be calm if everything is lost?
The blue mountains in the distance are being gently touched
     by the shade.
The icy pallor of an underwater wind
is sketching the contours of distant towers,
brightening eyes which are well defined and near,
but impossible as a trace of shady greenery suggesting
the hidden bed of an underground river.
Strike the lute, because voices
would break the evening air.
Let fingers set free, between the frets,
the unanimous weeping of things,
but never again let anyone attempt to strum the roots of life,
whose last sparks, with the setting sun, are about to cast
the rainbow colors of the music
on the yellow leaves,
and the sylvan gods are calling for silence in the thicket.
Let no one try to find out the notes
where they began.

          Night is falling
like dead leaves in the still fountain basins,
and with a gentle hand, presses down upon the elements of
     the music:
polished brass of the trumpets,
resonances which close their corolla around the bucranes
garlanded with ribbons and grapes.
Now the many-haloed lights
are sliding down the front steps

(¿Y por qué no subir, si todo está perdido?)
y se desgrana el vals entre las risas
mientras las lentejuelas de las máscaras
reflejan un brillante remolino de sedas,
como un enorme espejo alucinado.

(And why not go up, if all is lost?)
and the waltz is crumbling among laughing voices
while the spangles of the masks,
like an enormous trick mirror,
reflect a brilliant whirlwind of silks.

*Translated by John DuVal*

*Sketch of Death* (1967)

# ◆ PLAZA DE ITALIA

*De Chirico*

Es tan sólo una geografía de dormidos cadáveres de níquel lo
    que se nos ha concedido.
Una anatomía trazada por imborrables cuchillos de luna.
Como los ojos extrañamente sorprendidos—a pesar de una
    tenue indiferencia que recuerda el paso de los siglos—
de las muchachas apoyadas en el pretil de los puentes en los
    primeros días de las postguerras,
en la noche estancada todas las cosas detienen el delirio de
    sus límites
como el puñado de pequeños objetos y baratijas que sobre
    una manta
—dedales, alfileteros y flores de papel—
ancianas de ojos opacos venden en las plazas los días de
    fiesta,
aseguran al viajero que están recién fregadas las losas de la
    plaza
y que podrá, entre los pórticos abiertos a todos los caminos
    de la tierra,
extender sobre las piedras pulidas por el vaho de la luna
el reducido bagaje de su amor no correspondido, de su
    soledad vieja como el mundo,
el reducido puñado de figurillas y papeles arrugados
con los que comerciar quizás un poco de calor compartido,
que podrá rodear despacio y abrazar con sus ojos esa frágil
    reciedumbre de las cosas
que, por una vez, en el tiempo detenido, van a ser su
    patrimonio.
Sí, van a ser su patrimonio, como la paloma que aquel niño
    grabado en la piedra

# ◆ ITALY SQUARE

*De Chirico*


All we've been given is a landscape of sleeping, nickel
corpses.
An anatomy traced by indelible knives made of moon.
Like the strangely surprised eyes—in spite of a slight
indifference that recalls the passing of centuries—
of the girls leaning on bridge railings during the first days of
postwars,
in the stagnant night all things stop the delirium of their
limits
like the fistful of small objects and trinkets on a blanket
—thimbles, pincushions and paper flowers—
which old women with opaque eyes sell in the square on
holidays,
they assure the traveler that the stones in the square are
freshly scrubbed
and, between the porticos open to all the roads of the earth,
he might spread out on the stones polished by the vapor of
the moon
the reduced baggage of his unrequited love, of his loneliness
as old as the world,
the reduced handful of figurines and crumpled papers
he might trade for a little shared warmth,
and he could walk around them slowly and his eyes embrace
that fragile strength which things have
that, for once, held in time, will be his patrimony.
Yes, they'll be his patrimony, like the dove which the child
engraved in the stone

acercó a su boca a la hora de morir,
como los labios de las modelos lacerados sobre los carteles
un día cualquiera al amanecer, mientras la luna detiene sus
   carámbanos
sobre las losas de esta plaza, arrullando
la sombra detenida de los arcos y el mármol pulido de las
   columnas,
arrullando los arcos hasta el sueño.

brought near his mouth at the hour of his death,
like the lips of the models mangled on signs
any day at dawn, while the moon holds its icicles
above the stones of this square, humming
to the paused shadow of the arches and the polished marble
  of the columns,
humming the arches to sleep.


*Sketch of Death* (1967)

# ◆ EL EMBARCO PARA CYTEREA

*Sicut dii eritis.*

GEN. III, 4

Hoy que la triste nave está al partir,
con su espectacular monotonía,
quiero quedarme en la ribera, ver
confluir los colores en un mar de ceniza
y mientras tenuemente tañe el viento
las jarcias y las crines de los grifos dorados
oír lejanos en la oscuridad
los remos, los fanales, y estar solo.
Muchas veces la vi partir de lejos,
sus bronces y brocados y sus juegos de música:
el brillante estentor
de un ritual de gracias escondidas
y una sabiduría tan vieja como el mundo.
La vi tomar el largo
ligera bajo un dulce cargamento de sueños,
sueños que no envilecen y que el poder rescata
del laberinto de la fantasía,
y las pintadas muecas de las máscaras
un lujo alegre y sabio,
no atributos del miedo y el olvido.
También alguna vez hice el viaje
intentando creer y ser dichoso
y repitiendo al golpe de los remos:
aquí termina el reino de la muerte.
Y no guardo rencor
sino un deseo inhábil que no colman
las acrobacias de la voluntad,
y cierta ingratitud no muy profunda.

# ◆ SETTING SAIL FOR CYTHERA

*Sicut dii eritis.*

Gen. 3:4


Now that the sad ship is about to leave
with spectacular monotony,
I want to stay on the bank and watch
the colors flow together on a sea of ash,
and while the wind plays softly
on the riggings and the golden manes of the griffins,
to hear, far away in the dark,
the oars and the lighthouse bells, and be alone.
Many times, a long way off, I watched her setting sail
with her bronzes and brocades and her musical games:
the bright proclamation
of a ritual of hidden graces
and a wisdom as old as the earth.
I saw her take to the open sea,
light with her cargo of dreams,
dreams that don't corrupt, that power ransoms
from the labyrinth of fantasy,
and the painted grins of masks—
a lighthearted and wise exuberance,
not fear and forgetting.
And sometimes I even made the journey,
trying to believe and be happy
and repeating to the rhythm of the oars:
This is the end of the reign of death.
I don't hold a grudge,
just an ineffectual longing
which no acrobatics of the will can satisfy,
and a certain not-very-profound ingratitude.

*Translated by John DuVal*

*Sketch of Death* (1967)

# ◆ INVESTIGACION DE
# UNA DOBLE METONIMIA

Quien concibió la gloria de estos muros
amaba más la vida.        La elevación del cerro
revela y rige la función del lago:
invertir las imágenes y su apariencia plácida.
El negro nigromante al umbral de la gruta,
el eremita, la sombra de Quirón
acordando su andar como se ignoran.
Del otro lado la concreta estampa
sin la indulgencia de la alegoría
pero más esplendor; los encajes del hierro,
el jardincillo de los Conciertos Sacros,
la tenue batahola de la máquina hidráulica
que suenan para ti.        La música distante
las risas y el sudor y la reyerta
nunca serán tu historia
y suenan para ti.        Tu sangre crece
no en la persecución, por su relato,
y así desdices sombras que sin tú conocerlas
habitan ante ti, no su despojo
que despierta tu carne.        Y hasta inventas
para asirlas extremos
de precisa dicción, es tu literatura
no menos conocida, perseguidor de sombras,
retórico brillante
en tu recinto oscuro.        Y tuvo libertad.

## ◆ RESEARCH INTO
## A DOUBLE METONYMY

Whoever conceived the glory of these walls
loved life the most.
        The height of the hill
reveals and rules the function of the lake:
to invert the images and their placid appearance.
The black necromancer at the door of the cave,
the hermit, the shadow of Chiron
their steps concerting a mutual unawareness.
From the other side, the exact print
without the grace of the allegory
but with more splendor; the iron railings,
the little garden of the Sacred Concerts,
the subtle clatter of the hydraulic machine
that sound for you.
        The distant music
the laughter and the sweat and the quarrel
will never be your story
and they sound for you.
        Your blood grows
not in the pursuit, but in its telling,
and this way you contradict shadows that without your
   knowing them
stand before you, not their relic
that arouses your flesh.
        And you even create
extremes of precise diction
to seize them, your literature
is no less known, pursuer of shadows,
brilliant rhetorician
in your dark enclosure.
        And he was free.

*Scipio's Dream* (1971)

# ◆ PAESTUM

Los dioses nos observan desde la geometría
que es su imagen.
    Sus templos no temen a la luz
sino que en ella erigen el fulgor
de su blancura: columnatas
patentes contra el cielo y su resplandor límpido.
Existen en la luz.
    Así los pueblos bárbaros
intuyen el tumulto de sus dioses grutescos
que son ecos forjados en una sima oscura:
un chocar de guijarros en un túnel vacío.

Aquí los dioses son,
como la concepción de estas columnas,
un único placer: la inteligencia,
con su progenie de fantasmas lúcidos.

# ◆ PAESTUM

The gods observe us from geometry
which is their image.
                    Their temples do not fear the light
but erect the radiancy
of their whiteness in it: colonnades
patent against the sky and its limpid splendor.
They exist in the light.
                    This is how the barbarians
perceive the tumult of their cavernous gods
who are echoes forged in a dark cave:
a crashing together of pebbles in an empty tunnel.

Here the gods are—
like the conception of these columns—
a single pleasure: intelligence,
with its progeny of lucid ghosts.


*Variations and Figurations on a Theme of La Bruyère* (1974)

## ◆ VARIACIÓN IV
## DAD LIMOSNA A BELISARIO

### I

Durante muchos años la casa se asentó en tierra firme
estrechándola bajo su peso, y creció con ella
y la tierra cuarteada en estío por el desplome de sus músicas
miraba entre torrentes de luz derramarse las fuentes;
así al mirarla desde lejos surgía en la memoria
el despliegue de las horas pasadas, la sucesión
de las habitaciones y los objetos con su historia.
Apresar el calor de un instante es haber vivido
durante mucho tiempo en una inmensa casa:
abandonarla un día hacia un país extraño
y trasladar los muebles por el jardín desierto
mientras quedan atrás los muros con su historia,
el sonido del mar y las gamas del aire.
Y sólo lo vacío sobrevive: los objetos menudos,
lo que se puede trasladar y transmitir a otros;
el pasado permanece atrás, inseparable
del lugar en que tuvo vida, desplomado en el tiempo
con su magnificencia de cadáver antiguo
que al tocarlo se desmorona en una nube de polvo,
acumulación de joyas sin sentido
que luego redisponen otros, parodiando
con mascarillas, pectorales y ajorcas los contornos de un
	cuerpo.
Apresar el calor de un instante es
producir in día de ovlido el deleznable milagro
de recomponer el recuerdo con sus límites,
oficiar para otros el triunfo de la ausencia.

# ◆ VARIATION IV
## GIVE ALMS TO BELISARIUS

### I

For many years the house sat on firm ground
pressing it beneath its weight, and it grew with it
and the ground in summer cracked by the tumbling down of
   its music
watched the fountains overflow midst torrents of light;
and seeing it from afar, the unfolding of past hours
rose up in the memory, the succession
of rooms and objects with their history.
To grasp the warmth of an instant is to have lived
for a long time in an immense house:
to abandon it one day for a strange land
and move the furniture through the deserted garden
while the walls with their history are left behind,
the sound of the sea and the gammas of air.
And only the void remains: the small objects,
that can be carried away and handed on to others;
the past stays behind, inseparable
from the place where it found life, tumbling down in time
with the magnificence of an ancient cadaver
that when touched crumbles in a cloud of dust,
meaningless accumulation of jewels
that others will then rearrange, parodying
the outline of a body with masks, breast plates and anklets.
To grasp the warmth of an instant is
to produce, one forgotten day, the fragile miracle
of recomposing the memory with its limits,
to officiate the triumph of absence for others.

Para otros, porque quien asiste a su muerte diaria
al envejecimiento de la piel y su memoria,
es ajeno a la liturgia de conseguir frente al papel
con sus trastos de buhonero una ilusión de vida
coloreada y presente como un Museo de Cera,
esa evidencia de realidad que sólo en el lenguaje existe
y se traslada en el tiempo rellenándolo
con su carnalidad de serrín y de seda,
creando para lo pasado colores y sentido,
una entidad, incluso, de que no gozó nunca
más que ahora, convertido en un brillante simulacro
el fastuoso fraude en que el tiempo se anula;
si es que el tiempo existió: si es que no es ahora
real, más que entonces acaso, lo que el tiempo destruye,
si es que no produce el lenguaje sus propios fantasmas
que proyectados hacia atrás inventan una realidad posible
de que ellos serían reflejo, puesto que de la nada
nada se engendre, y hasta el torpe cadáver que las palabras
  hilan
ha de ser hijo de una realidad anterior en el tiempo.
La casa permanece lejos, los ojos no la saben
y la memoria y la piel interrogadas
responden a su idea con un vasto silencio;
y un día volvemos a ella, contemplamos el pórtico:
de nada es capaz la piel entonces; los muros son distintos.
Y por qué pueda ser el poema lugar de una epifanía
que la piel y los ojos ignoran, salvación de la muerte
que proclaman la piel y los ojos con su silencio oscuro,
dejando a las palabras su miserable tráfico.


## II

Hemos puesto en cuestión numerosas gramáticas,
leído hasta la saciedad la experiencia de otros
y en fotografías borrosas perseguido su imagen
inquiriendo un volumen para sus gestos planos,
codiciosos de aquello de que era razonable

For others, because the one who attends its daily death,
the aging of the skin and its memory,
is foreign to the liturgy of creating an illusion of life,
on paper, with peddler's trappings,
colored and present like a Wax Museum,
that evidence of reality which only exists in language
and is moved through time stuffed
with its flesh of sawdust and silk,
creating colors and meaning for the past,
an entity which, in fact, it never enjoyed
any more than now, the pompous fraud when time's
    annulled
changed into a shining simulacrum;
if time existed at all: if now, more than then perhaps,
what time destroys isn't real,
if language does not produce its own phantoms
that projected backwards invent a possible reality
of which they'd be a reflection, since nothing is born
out of nothing, and even the torpid body that words weave
must be the child of a former reality in time.
The house remains at a distance, eyes do not know it
and the memory and skin when questioned
respond to the idea of it with vast silence;
and one day we go back to it, we contemplate the doorway:
the skin can do nothing then; the walls are different.
And how can the poem be the place for an epiphany
of which skin and eyes are unaware, salvation from the death
that the skin and eyes proclaim with their dark silence,
leaving to words their miserable trade.


## II


We've questioned numerous grammars,
satiated ourselves with reading the experiences of others
and pursued their image in blurred photographs
researching a volume for their essential traits,
desirous of that from which one might reasonably

esperar sabiduría, para obtener al fin
un pobre patrimonio de terrenos baldíos,
una corta colección de medallas y cintas
símbolo de triunfos que ya nadie recuerda,
juguetes con encaje sucio cuyos ojos hundidos
remiten a una infancia convencional y anónima;
y nos devuelve a ellos la vanidad del coleccionista
que dice poseer con los objetos su alma; nos miran
con fijeza de búhos disecados desde la redondez de su urna:
una apariencia que es muerte y serrín y grandes ojos de
   vidrio.

Las palabras nos envuelven en su manto de plomo,
nos inmovilizan las manos con su cetro
mientras la perspectiva de las gruesas columnas
percute nuestros ojos en un punto preciso.
Como perseguirlas fue un viaje por mar hacia las tierras
   vírgenes,
cielos de color distinto y animales de fábula,
y un día devuelven las olas el cadáver de un ahogado,
recubierto de algas oscuras, con las órbitas huecas;
arrojado a la luz, mira la fiesta de los sentidos
y otras naves que parten, como un huésped
procedente de un país donde todo es silencio.

expect wisdom, to obtain in the end
a poor patrimony of wastelands,
a partial collection of medals and ribbons
the symbol of triumphs no one remembers now,
toys with dirty lace whose sunken eyes
remit to a conventional, anonymous childhood;
and the vanity of the collector who claims to possess the soul
    with the object
takes us back to them; they watch us
from the roundness of their case with the fixed stare of
    dissected owls:
a look that is death and sawdust and large glass eyes.

Words wrap us up in their mantle of lead,
they immobilize our hands with their sceptre
while the perspective of the thick columns
strikes our eyes on a precise point.
As if pursuing them was a voyage by sea towards virgin
    lands,
skies of a different color and storybook animals,
and one day the waves return the body of a drowned man,
covered with dark algae, and with the eye sockets empty;
thrown towards the light, he watches the feast of the senses
and other departing ships—like a visitor
from a country where it's all silence.

*Variations and Figurations on a Theme of La Bruyère* (1974)

# ◆ VII
# EL AZAR OBJETIVO

Así pues él camina por un tiempo vacío,
espectador de formas y volúmenes
entre presencias que no ve.
                    No hablo de las grandes líneas,
que ésas sí están a nuestro alcance, y así corre el alero
en grandes hemiciclos que remata
la tangente lejana de algún río;
pero no es más que un trazo de buril
en la imaginación, como partir un plano
con una cruz que patentiza en partes
que la materia es; y aun así vacua,
pues le finge espejismos de su zumbido, absorto
en encubrir cómo oculta su ley.
                    Cuando vacía
esa memoria voluntaria, como chamarilero
se cree en posesión del pasado, puesto que los escombros,
ya que del pasado proceden, le coloquen
ahora en situación de vivirlo.
                    Y con todo
palpa ausencias que achaca no a nulidad del procedimiento
sino a limitación de la memoria,
olvido de algún fragmento significativo que ponga
en solución aquella maquinaria,
o bien a su impericia combinatoria, que hubiera
de suplirlo, ante un número suficiente aunque corto
de datos dispersos.
                    Depende,
aunque lo ignora, de una sola pisada que, sonando,
los desordene, y concluya de ese modo en azar su imagen
    cierta;

# ◆ OBJECTIVE CHANCE

So he's walking through a void in time,
a spectator of forms and volumes
among presences he cannot see.
   I'm not speaking of the greater lines,
those are certainly at our reach, and the eaves runs like this
in large semicircles finished off
by the tangent of some distant river;
but it's nothing more than the mark of a burin
in the imagination, like dividing a plane
with a cross that proves by the parts
that the material is; and even empty,
it feigns to him mirages of its humming, absorbed
in hiding how the law is concealed.
                     When he empties out
the voluntary memory, like a secondhand dealer
he thinks he's in possession of the past, since the debris,
coming of course from the past, may place him
now in a position to live it.
                And even so
he notes something missing, which he blames not on the
    nullity of the method
but on limitations of memory,
the omission of some meaningful fragment that might hold
the solution to that mechanism,
or perhaps to its combinative ineptitude, that ought
to be expanded, given a small yet sufficient number
of dispersed facts.
           It depends,
although he doesn't know it, on a single step that, sounding,
may disarrange them, and his certain image may thus fall to
    chance;

GUILLERMO CARNERO   165

resonando en el empedrado de un pasadizo estrecho
dicte un ritmo a la memoria, y su cochambre
se anule, suscitando los reales fantasmas,
derogación del fetichismo tácito que llamamos «presente»
cuyo prestigio vulneran los enigmas
que, invadiendo la memoria, suscita el azar, y a veces
resuelve.

resounding on the stone pavement of a narrow passage
it may prescribe a rhythm to the memory, wiping away
the grime and arousing the real ghosts,
derogation of the tacit fetishism that we call "present"
whose prestige is discredited by enigmas
that chance, invading the memory, awakens and sometimes
  resolves.

*Objective Chance* (1975)

# DISCURSO DE
# LA SERVIDUMBRE VOLUNTARIA

¿Por qué dejarle puertas al azar
y que pueda verter su fauna entonces,
inundar el tiempo vacío con sus reptiles y el rosáceo
ondear de las membranas de sus peces?
El tiempo como un espacio oblongo sin principio ni grietas
ni recodos o aristas en donde hallar refugio,
que gira sobre su eje con gravidez de pecera
cuando ovilla en el aire circunvoluciones de noria.
Ninguna de sus puertas es distinta,
como en la Sala Oval de un Parque de Atracciones,
y una sola conduce al jardincillo mágico;
caemos, como en *Viaje al centro de la Tierra,*
y ya no es el tiempo discurrir con la nariz contra el cristal
sino penetrar hacia dentro, y saber. ¿Por qué dejar esto al
    azar?
A lo cual podría objetarse que él es el único barquero.
Pero si el preciso adagio con que la puerta abre,
en vez de encontrado al azar entre mil combinaciones
    posibles
sustitutivas, hubiera sido
*provocado*, por así decirlo, ¿no tendría
efectos similares? Y el conocer veinticinco lenguas como
    Mitrídates,
¿es parte del azar, o bien posee una función contraria?
El origen de la creación es miserable:
un olor de alquitrán o de tierra mojada,
el gotear de la lluvia en un alero,
el perfume de siempre en un cuello distinto
o un gesto de estupor en el cuarto de baño.

# ◆ DISCOURSE ON
# VOLUNTARY SERVITUDE

Why leave doors open to chance
and allow it then to spill its fauna,
to flood vacant time with reptiles and rose-like
waves of fish membranes?
Time like an oblong space without a beginning or cracks
or corners or angles where refuge might be found,
that spins on its axis with the fullness of a fishbowl
while winding norial circumvolutions in the air.
None of its doors is different,
like in the Mirror Maze of an Amusement Park,
and only one leads to the small, magic garden;
we fall, like in *Voyage to the Center of the Earth*,
and time is no longer thinking with your nose pressed
    against the glass
but pressing in, and knowing. Why leave it up to chance?
To which one might object that he is the only boatsman.
But if the exact adagio with which the door opens,
instead of found perchance from a thousand possible
    combinations
all interchangeable, had been
*provoked*, to put it that way, wouldn't the effect
be similar? And knowing twenty-five languages, like
    Mithridates,
is that part of chance, or does it possess an opposite
    function?
The origin of creation is miserable:
a smell of tar or damp earth,
the dripping of rain in a gutter,
the same old perfume on a different neck
or a stupefied look in the bathroom.

Recoger al azar
la esquirla imaginaria de un gran rompecabezas
pisoteado, y darle veracidad escénica.
Conferirle de nuevo su realidad.
                                    Qué es
su realidad; un depósito de odio
que otro día nos lleva a intentar rehacer
su realidad. ¿Es realidad
el poso de papel indefenso, injuriado
en un pobre ejercicio? El odio sí es real;
la formulación de toda nostalgia es imprecisa
y, en suma, un homenaje al fácil expediente
del conjuro luminoso de la noria,
creador de feraces tensiones entre sumisión y rechazo
de las que surge la fumarola lírica.
                                    Este poema
carece incluso de ese heroísmo plácido:
realidad, negación de realidad,
*ça sonne creux sous la lime.*
                        El odio sí es real;
la abstracción erradica todo sentido trágico,
persiste en inexistir para mejor señalar un síntoma
y apunta como el dedo acusador de la estatua de Casio, pero
      muda
como ella, así que si el decorado le cambian se convierte
de acusadora en acusada, por su disponibilidad potencial
para señalar cualquier cosa, y no se alteran
sus ojos mudos y sapientes, de dura piedra impávidos
receptivos de injuria—
                        Es un discurso muerto,
el esqueleto ritual que ironiza la fe
en la virtud de la ironía,
embadurnado de sangre para indicar resurrección.

El vaporcillo inquieta la placidez del lago,
araña el firmamento de la ciudad inmersa.
La lámpara de aceite pone un halo cobrizo
sobre la piel mojada y los labios sedosos;

      To gather up haphazardly
the imaginary splinter of a great, trampled jigsaw puzzle,
and give it theatrical veracity.
To give it back its reality.
       What is
its reality; a depository of hate
that another day leads us to remake
its reality. Is reality
the scraps of defenseless paper, injured
in a paltry exercise? Hate is real indeed;
the formulation of all nostalgia is inexact
and, in summary, a homage to the easy expediency
of the luminous incantation of the waterwheel,
creator of fruitful tensions between submission and rejection
from which the lyric fumarole springs.
        This poem
lacks even that peaceful heroism:
reality, negation of reality,
*ça sonne creux sous la lime.*
      Hate is real indeed;
abstraction eradicates any tragic meaning,
it persists in nonexisting to better indicate a symptom
and points like the accusing finger of the statue of Cassius,
  but dumb
like it, so that if they change the decor, it changes
from accuser to accused, because of its potential
  disposability
for pointing at anything, and its dumb and knowing eyes
never change, hard, stone, dauntless
receptacles of injury—
      It's a dead discourse,
the ritual skeleton that renders faith
in the virtue of irony ironic,
bedaubed with blood to suggest resurrection.

Fog disturbs the peacefulness of the lake,
scratches the firmament of the sunken city.
The oil lamp makes a coppery halo
on the wet skin and silky lips;

al tenderse la mano tiene que desgarrar
el rugoso murmullo de la fosforescencia.
A mi lado se tiende un espectro de jade
veteado de barro y ceñido de algas
mientras el mar proyecta sobre el cielo nuboso
la fantasmagoría de la ciudad yacente,
como un espejo. Miro las cúpulas aéreas,
los hoteles lumínicos arrasados de música,
la gran arquitectura que con leve sonrisa
me hace reconocer el húmedo cadáver
que comparte la cama.
                      En noches como ésta
está de pie, solemne, junto al ojo de buey;
con un puntero nombra a las constelaciones:
«Aquí, la habitación resonante de risa;
la veranda en silencio con sus cristales rotos;
el *Bar Rosa*—jugosos y blancos canapés
envueltos en pulcras hojas de lechuga—;
la carretera oscura junto al funicular;
el comedor del *Rana Verde*.»
                      Me concedes el barro
en que reside el don de la palabra.
                      Tu me donnes ta boue,
jeune fille qui apporte le miroir.

a stretched out hand must tear
the wrinkled murmur of the phosphorescence.
A specter of jade, streaked with mud
and wrapped in algae, stretches out at my side
while the sea projects on the clouded sky
the phantasmagoria of the recumbent city,
like a mirror. I look at the cupolas of the sky,
the shiny hotels filled up with music,
the great architecture that with a slight smile
makes me recognize the humid cadaver
that shares my bed.
              On nights like this
it stands, solemn, next to the ox-eye;
with a pointer it names the constellations:
"Here, the room resounding with laughter;
the veranda in silence with its broken windows;
the *Rose Bar*—juicy, white canapés
wrapped in pretty lettuce leaves—;
the dark road next to the funicular;
the dining room of the *Green Frog*."
                    You give me the clay
that holds the gift of words.
              Tu me donnes ta boue,
jeune fille qui apporte le miroir.


*Testing a Theory of Vision* (1979)

# ◆ LE GRAND JEU

*"Et icelui paradis doit estre fait*
*de papier au dedens duquel doit avoir*
*branches d'arbres, les ung fleuriz, les*
*autres chargés de fruitz de plusieurs*
*espèces comme cerises, poires, pommes,*
*figues, raisins et telles choses*
*artificiellement faictes . . ."*

Manuscrit de la Résurrection,
anónimo siglo xv. París, Bibl. Nat.

Lugares luminosos de otro tiempo, teñidos
por la capacidad de sufrir daño
en los que el mar rabiosamente yerra
exaltando el despojo en que se mece
la podrida guirnalda de las horas.
El faro triza y lame la mudez de los muros,
desteñido tapiz donde campean
dioses semiborrados y gozosos,
entre los atributos del fervor y del miedo.
Vuelven las estaciones a hendir el horizonte,
idéntica blancura que inexorable inflige
a las mismas arenas un cielo no distinto;
el lastre funeral de las imágenes
regresa a la espesura, y su fulgor se apaga.
Sobre su liviandad se desmorona
el color y milagro de la línea,
cúpula de cristal sobre muros de humo.
Aún puedo disponer tres especies de azul
si pienso este lugar: en la sombra del cabo
una llaga violeta que deriva hacia el gris
por amenaza del amanecer,
y un hilillo lechoso sobre el banco de arena.
Eso es lo que he sabido
conservar: una pobre
sutileza cromática.

# ◆ LE GRAND JEU

"*Et icelui paradis doit estre fait
de papier au dedens duquel doit avoir
branches d'arbres, les ung fleuriz, les
autres chargés de fruitz de plusieurs
espèces comme cerises, poires, pommes,
figues, raisins et telles choses
artificiellement faictes . . .*"

*Manuscrit de la Résurrection,*
anonymous, XV Cent. Paris, Natl. Lib.

Bright places of another time, colored
by a capacity for suffering harm
where the sea flows angrily
raising up the spoils where the withered
garland of the hours rocks back and forth.
The lighthouse breaks and licks the dumbness of the walls,
discolored tapestry where joyful, partly faded gods walk
    about
between the attributes of fervor and fear.
The seasons return to break up the horizon,
the identical whiteness that relentlessly inflicts
a not different sky on the same sands;
the funeral weight of the images
comes back to the thicket, and its brilliancy goes out.
Above its weightlessness, the color
and the miracle of the line crumble down,
a glass dome above walls of smoke.
I can still place three shades of blue
if I think about this spot: in the shadow of the promontory
a violet wound that goes into the gray
with the threat of dawn,
and a milky thread above the sandy bank.
That's what I've known how to save: a pitiful
chromatic subtlety.

GUILLERMO CARNERO  175

Silencio de la noche
en que la luna tiende sobre el agua
una cuerda de luz que al oscilar resuena
de un lado a otro del paisaje cóncavo,
o bien en un lenguaje llanamente poético:
las dos mil campanillas de la Torre
de la Felicidad—
          Felicidad:
aroma de la llama de romero,
columnilla de humo hacia el fondo del valle,
sonar de cornamusas en otoño,
límpido, puro y claro ritornelo
por una montaña rusa de helado de caramelo,
TEMPLUM SUPER CLOACAM
          *Pitié pour nos erreurs.*

Una capa finísima que mancha el paisaje
o lo conserva embalsamado
como en espera de la resurrección
que no sucederá. O sí: los cráneos mondos,
la negra raja sobre el vientre hueco,
el sordo ruido con que la piel del codo
se rompe en el esfuerzo de emerger
de la tierra—
          pero aquí no hay terror;
un estratega sin convencimiento
que manipula el diorama
ya previsto: la casa junto al mar,
el sol resplandeciente con una gran sonrisa
anaranjada, en el jardín las fieras
jugueteando panza arriba
con el volante de un vestido—y por la noche
la blanca torrecilla de papel
despierta la sonrisa de las rubias sirenas.
Inevitablemente el antiguo Misterio
da fin, la historia es poco variable,

Silence of the night
when the moon hangs a string of light
above the water, that swinging from side to side
resounds through the concave landscape,
or perhaps in a fully poetic language:
the two thousand bells of the Tower
of Happiness—
                    Happiness:
aroma of a rosemary flame,
a slender column of smoke towards the bottom of the valley,
the sound of bagpipes in Fall,
limpid, pure and clear refrain
on a rollercoaster of caramel ice cream,
TEMPLUM SUPER CLOACAM
                              *Pitié pour nos erreurs.*

A thin, thin layer that stains the landscape
or keeps it preserved
as if waiting for a resurrection
that will not happen. Or rather: the clean skulls,
the black gash above the empty belly,
the muffled sound of the elbow skin
breaking as it forces up
from the ground—
                    but there's no terror here;
a strategist without conviction
who manipulates the prearranged diorama:
the house near the sea,
the resplendent sun with a big, orange smile,
in the garden the wild beasts
rolling on their backs
and playing with the ruffle of a dress—and in the night
a small, white, paper tower
awakens the smiles of the blond sirens.
Inevitably the old Mystery
comes to an end, the story hardly varies,

GUILLERMO CARNERO   177

y las figuras del retablo
van perdiendo color. El tema es siempre el mismo.
Una delgada capa de imágenes previstas
ensucia el paisaje, y después unas líneas
ensucian el papel.
Resumiendo: invertir
el proceso creador; no de la emoción al poema
sino al contrario.
*Pitié pour nos erreurs.*

and the statues of the altarpiece
go on losing their color. It's always the same theme.
A thin layer of foreseen images
spoils the landscape, and then some verses
spoil the page.
To sum up: invert
the creative process; not from the emotion to the poem
but vice versa.
*Pitié pour nos erreurs.*

*Testing a Theory of Vision* (1979)

# ◆ OSTENDE

*Obediencia me lleva y no osadía.*

VILLAMEDIANA


*Nuestros burgueses . . . sienten una*
*grandísima fruición en seducirse*
*unos a otros sus mujeres.*

Manifiesto Comunista, II

Recorrer los senderos alfombrados
de húmedas y esponjadas hojas muertas,
no por la arista gris de grava fría
como la hoja de un cuchillo.
                                    Mueven
su ramaje los plátanos como sábanas lentas
empapadas de noche, de grávida humedad
y reluciente.
                    También en la espesura
late la oscuridad de las cavernas
y el sol sobre las hojas evapora
las gotas de rocío—
                            el aura de calor
que envuelve e ilumina los cuerpos agotados
cuando duermen: si acercas la mejilla
ves las formas bailar y retorcerse,
un espejismo fácil y sin riesgo:
dos bueyes que remontan la colina,
el mago que construye laberintos,
el calafate, el leproso, el halconero
parten seguros al amanecer,
no como yo, por los senderos
cubiertos de hojas muertas, esponjadas y húmedas.
A veces entre los árboles clarean
los lugares amenos que conozco:
el pintado vaporcillo con su blanca cabeza

# ◆ *OSTEND*

*Obedience, not boldness, guides me.*

VILLAMEDIANA

*Our bourgeois men . . . find*
*great fulfillment in seducing*
*each other's wives.*

The Communist Manifesto, II

Travel the carpeted paths
of dead, soaked leaves,
not the gray, gravel side, cold
like the blade of a knife.
                    The plane trees
slowly move their leaves like sheets
soaked with night, damp through
and shining.
              And in the thick woods,
the darkness of the caverns throbs
and the sun on the leaves dries up
the drops of dew—
                    the aura of warmth
wrapping round and brightening tired bodies
as they sleep: if you bring your cheek close
you can see the shapes dancing and twisting,
an easy, safe illusion:
two oxen going up the hill,
the magus constructing labyrinths,
the shipwright, the leper and the falconer
go out boldly at dawn,
not as I, along the paths
strewn with dead, soaked leaves.
Sometimes the lovely spots I know
come to light among the trees:
the little, painted steamboat with its white,

GUILLERMO CARNERO   181

de ganso, acribillada de remaches y cintas;
las olas estrellándose bajo el suelo de tablas
del gran salón de baile abandonado,
las lágrimas de hielo que lloran los tritones
emergiendo en la nieve de las fuentes heladas;
el cuartito en reposo con la cama deshecha
junto al enorme anuncio de neón
que lanza sobre el cuerpo reflejos verdes, rojos,
como en las pesadillas de los viejos opiómanos
del siglo diecinueve.
                Un cervatillo salta
impasible: lo sigo.
                En un claro del bosque
está sentada al borde de la fuente,
con blanquísima túnica que no ofrece materia
que desgarrar a la rama del espino.
Corro tras ella sin saber su rostro,
pero no escapa sino que conduce
hasta lo más espeso de la fronda,
donde juntos rodamos entre las hojas muertas.
Cuando la estrecho su rostro se ha borrado,
la carne hierve y se diluye; el hueso
se convierte en un reguero de ceniza
y en medio de la forma que levemente humea
brilla nítida y pura una piedra preciosa.
La recojo y me arreglo la corbata;
de vuelta, silencioso en el vagón del tren,
temo que me delate su fulgor
que resplandece y quema aún bajo el abrigo.
Tengo una colección considerable
y en el silencio de mi biblioteca
las acaricio, las pulo, las ordeno
y a veces las imprimo.
En el dolor se engendra la conciencia.

Recorrer los senderos alfombrados
de húmedas y esponjadas hojas muertas,
inseguro paisaje poblado de demonios

goose-like head, riddled with bands and rivets;
the waves crashing beneath the planks
of the great, abandoned ballroom,
the icy tears the Tritons cry
emerging in the snow of the frozen fountains,
the little room at rest with an unmade bed
next to an enormous neon sign
casting green and red reflections on the body,
like in nightmares dreamt by opium-eaters
back in the nineteenth century.
                              A musk deer jumps
indifferently: I follow it.
                              In a clearing in the woods
a woman sits at the edge of the fountain,
wearing a very white tunic that has no substance
for the thornbush to catch.
I run after her not knowing her face,
but instead of fleeing she leads me
to the thickest part of the woods,
where we roll together in the dead leaves.
When I reach out for her, her face disappears
her flesh boils and melts; her bones
turn to a spot of ashes
and in the center of the faintly smoking form
a precious stone shines bright and pure.
I pick it up and straighten my tie;
on the way back, quiet in the car of the train,
I'm afraid its brilliance will give me away,
still shining and burning inside my coat.
I have a considerable collection
and in the silence of my study
I caress, polish and arrange them
and sometimes print them.
Consciousness is born out of pain.

Travel the carpeted paths
of dead, soaked leaves,
unsafe country full of demons

que adoptan apariencia de formas deseables
para perder al viajero.
　　　　　　　Mas no perecerá
quien sabe que no hay más que la palabra
al final del viaje.
　　　　　Por ella los lugares,
las camas, los crepúsculos y los amaneceres
en cálidos hoteles sitiados
forman una perfecta arquitectura
vacía y descarnada como duelas y ejes
de los modelos astronómicos.
Vacío perseguido cuya extensión no acaba
como es inagotable la conciencia,
la anchura de su río
y su profundidad.
　　　　　　Desde el balcón
veo romper las olas una a una,
con mansedumbre, sin pavor.
Sin violencia ni gloria se acercan a morir
las líneas sucesivas que forman el poema.
Brillante arquitectura que es fácil levantar
igual que las volutas, los pináculos,
las columnatas y las logias
en las que se sepulta una clase acabada
ostentando sus nobles materiales
tras un viaje en el vacío.
　　　　　　　Producir un discurso
ya no es signo de vida, es la prueba mejor
de su terminación.
　　　　　　En el vacío
no se engendra discurso,
pero sí en la conciencia del vacío.

that adopt the appearance of likeable forms
to put the traveler off course.
                            But those who know
that the word is the only thing at the journey's end
will not perish.
                    Through words, the places,
beds, twilights and dawns
besieged in warm hotels
form a perfect architecture
empty and fleshed like the staves and axles
of planetary models.
A pursued void whose limits do not end,
inexhaustible, like consciousness,
the width of its river
and its depth.
                    From the balcony
I see the waves breaking one by one,
gently, without fear.
With neither violence nor glory, the successive lines
that form the poem rise up and die.
A brilliant architecture that is easy to build
the same as the volutes, pinnacles,
the colonnades and the loggias
where a washed-up class is buried
with the ostent of its noble materials
after a trip through the void.
                            Composing a discourse
is no longer a sign of life, but the best proof
of its end.
                    Discourse isn't born
in the void,
but, yes, in our awareness of the void.


*Testing a Theory of Vision* (1979)

# ANTONIO COLINAS

*La Bañeza, 1946*

# ANTONIO
# COLINAS

Francisco Martínez García in his *Historia de la literatura leonesa* (History of Leonese Literature [1084−1113]) depicts Antonio Colinas's life by inscribing it in the landscapes which have added a dimension to his personal development and poetic vision: his native region, León, the ancient Latinized kingdom, which Colinas in his poetry would call by its Roman name, Castra Petavonium; Córdoba, the medieval capital of Arab Spain, where Colinas as a young man discovered poetry as a vocation; Madrid, the great metropolitan heart of Spain, where he pursued a university education in history and engineering and established important literary contacts; Italy, where he taught Spanish at the Universities of Milan and Bergamo and discovered a starkly different form of Latin culture, not cloistered and austere as in his native Castra Petavonium, but openly Latin; and finally Ibiza, lying in the Mediterranean between Spain and Italy, where he has lived since 1977, at a distance from the centers of cultural activity and fully dedicated to writing—poetry, narrative, criticism, and translation.

Although Colinas, born in 1946, is close in age to Guillermo Carnero and Pere Gimferrer, more often than not, he has been set apart from the *novísimos*. In the strictest sense of the word he is not a *novísimo*, since Castellet did not include him in his 1970 anthology, in spite of the fact that Colinas by that date had established his reputation as a promising young poet, with two collections published in 1969: *Poemas de la tierra y de la sangre*

(Poems of the Land and the Blood) and *Preludios a una noche total* (Preludes to a Total Night). Also, Colinas, in his own words, feels little affinity for the poetic criteria listed in Castellet's introduction, especially those concerned with media-transmitted mythologies.[1] Nonetheless, some of his attitudes towards poetry establish a common bond between him and other poets of his generation and, at the same time, set him at variance with the neo-realistic aesthetic of the forties and fifties. Despite the subtleties of their individual crafts—and each reveals a unique approach to poetry—Colinas, Gimferrer, Carnero, and Vázquez Montalbán would agree on several essential points: they all believe that poetry is not primarily communication—a common definition used by many postwar poets—but rather a form of knowledge; they dismiss the social or political function of poetry, agreeing, as Pound said, that what can be said in a good essay should not be expressed in a poor poem; and they are all interested not so much in apparent realities but in a deeper knowledge which transcends common, daily experience.

If we accept Carlos Bousoño's argument that metapoetics is fundamental to the verse of young Spanish poets in the seventies (27–30), then an important difference between Colinas and some poets of his generation must reside in the latter's infrequent reference to his medium. If he is at odds with language in any sense, he does not make it a problem to be explored in the poem. Only occasionally, as in the following lines from the poem "Caballos y molinos en el pinar" (Horses and Windmills in a Pine Grove), *Poesías, 1967–1981*, does he imply a possible lack of confidence in language:

> wood, flesh, water and stones,
> just as they are: material and sign of the Great Whole.
> Sign of something whole that has never been named to you,
> a real sign (not a dream, since you don't yet know how to dream),
> beautiful images in a broken mirror
> that no one, until now, has managed to unite
> harmoniously so as to calm the human part.
>
> $(175-76)$[2]

Here Colinas suggests that nature itself holds the most faithful testimony to nature and that linguistic images are inadequate when compared with the living, total, natural image. The inadequacy of words, however, never actually consolidates into what could be called a theme in Colinas's verse; it appears rather as a base for elegizing the unspoken revelations of the landscape, night, and other natural phenomena, towards which the poet must direct his vision.

As Colinas says in his preface to *Astrolabio* (Astrolabe), "Today I think that poetry is something like the pure and full testimony of feelings expressed upon the earth and among the stones, that is, in the space in which it's been our fortune to live, reduced to its greatest elementality" (7).[3]

Although, as theorist, Colinas has viewed poetry as a multifaceted concept and has often prefaced his definitions with the phrase, "poetry, among other things, is . . . ," as a poet he has consistently focused on natural space as a source of poetry and knowledge. He fixes his sight on the narrow confines of a specific landscape or the great, natural places of the planet or universe, such as the sea or "that eternal astral void" ("ese eterno vacío astral" *Astrolabio* 7). The night, by far his most sustained image, is, in Colinas's words, "that space without dates, without names where we ask the great questions, where we let out the great screams."[4] In the poem "Novalis" the poet addresses night as a source of inspiration and sensuous beauty. In many poems which treat a specific landscape, the geography itself may suggest a symbolic "route" whereby the poet arrives at knowledge. In "La Corona," for example, the poet's exploration of a mountain in his native León takes the form of a vertical ascent towards "barbarous heights" ("bárbaras alturas" [176]), words which perhaps suggest a profound and frightening knowledge of life. In "River of Shadow" the search is horizontal, along a "road lined with dour hundred-year-old fig trees" ("camino bordeado de abrumadoras higueras centenarias" [183]), possibly a metaphor for traditional beliefs.

In addition to the spatial or geographic dimension, the search for knowledge is also frequently given a temporal dimension, either specific or abstract. Time may enter the poem simply as a reference to something or someone from a remote era—an Etruscan tomb in "Sepulcher in Tarquinia," an ancient statue in "Head of the Goddess in My Hands," the dolphin myth in Canto VI of *Noche más allá de la noche* (Night Beyond Night), and, from that same collection, numerous references to historical or legendary characters, such as Ulysses and Penelope (Canto VIII) and the unnamed somnambulist of Araby (Canto XX). References to a less remote past include the aging Casanova ("Giacomo Casanova Accepts the Position of Librarian . . .") and Novalis from the poem by the same name.

In a more abstract sense, the temporal focus is maintained through language which emphasizes time, particularly time as a continuum of related moments. Colinas often employs adverbs of time, such as *then, now, before,* etc. He frequently uses the imperfect tense of the verb, i.e., *was speaking, used to speak,* which stresses continuity, progression, or repetition rather than termination. Likewise, the metrical structure of the verse produces a dramatic sense of movement in time. Although Colinas in his middle collections, *Sepulcro en Tarquinia* (1975) and *Astrolabio* (1979), experiments with free verse, he usually prefers either the eleven- or fourteen-syllable line, often divided into hemistiches. His rhythms are clearly lyrical rather than discursive. Generally he limits the structural breaks in the poem, either eliminating them altogether or dividing the poem into a few relatively long units. These factors help to establish a smooth, uninterrupted flow of words. Also, his language is both structurally and semantically unencumbered, thus permitting a more rapid reading of the poem. Unlike many contemporary poets, Colinas maintains a concurrence between grammatical and verse units, thereby allowing his readers to read quickly, unhindered by the possible ambiguities of frequent enjambment. All in all, the linguistic properties of his poetry carry readers forward rather than slowing them down.

Although Colinas accentuates the passage of time in his poetry, he has some poems that are static, like pauses within a larger context. The speakers of these poems are often people who for one reason or another are fleeing from activity or change, like the aging Casanova who seeks refuge in the Count of Waldstein's library, or the persona in "Novalis" who asks the spheres to come to a halt, or the one of "November in England" who finds a safe, insular place, away from the sea, for him a symbol of death. Sometimes the poet portrays works of art or architecture as special kinds of pauses, like frozen time, held still in art, or as beauty preserved in art and thus uncorrupted by time. In "Head of the Goddess," Colinas—reminiscent of Keats—writes: "Dark clay shapes your form / that holds time still" ("Barro oscuro conforma tu figura / que mantiene el tiempo detenido" [194]). A character in a poem may symbolize a pause in time, such as the somnambulist in Canto XX of *Noche más allá de la noche,* who says: "But time still comes to a halt and I am time" ("Pero aún se detiene el tiempo y yo soy tiempo" [283]). Canto XI portrays one of the most dramatic pauses in all of history, the eruption of Vesuvius, which brings the activity of an entire town to a sudden halt, turning Pompeii into an immense tomb of human activity.

Colinas's *Noche más allá de la noche* (Night Beyond Night), his last volume represented in this collection, communicates most clearly his notion of what the thematic and stylistic essentials of poetry might be: Nature, man's emotional response to Nature, and formal purity. The similarity between the titles of his early volume, *Preludios a una noche total,* and this last one indicates the unitary nature of his collected poetry and attests to his belief, in agreement with Rilke, that "poetry is a process of purification and growth" (54).[5] In retrospect, his earlier works move towards a "night beyond night," his goal having been to refine conceptual essences and to create images which explore or express these essences. In this respect, night evolves into a symbol of the universe or the void, and the poet's role becomes the act of contemplating and, if possible, penetrating that "eternal astral void" (quoted above).

This particular vision of the poet, so aptly concretized by Leopardi's shepherd or wanderer seated on a rock and staring up at the stars (*Leopardi* 91–2), provides a general context or backdrop against which the visions of individual poems might be portrayed. The many fragments of time and space, like individual segments of a story, eventually form a clean, unbroken line, and poetry transcends specific experience to become a succession of timeless moments. The individual events do not go out of the poem but rather find their place within an historical progression. I would also maintain, and this I believe to be applicable to Colinas's poetry in general, that the events themselves are less significant than the speakers' emotional responses to them. In this sense, the poems of *Noche más allá de la noche* form not a chronicle of events but rather a history of consciousness in which the poet recreates the consciousness of many individuals, both real and fictional, who have figured in a collective experience. Even when the individuals in question are specific—Casanova, Novalis, Ulysses, and others—their positions lend themselves to a more universal application.

These poetic essentials—Nature, man's response to Nature, and formal purity—which Colinas has sought with fervor and constancy, distinguish him from many poets of the third postwar generation, including Gimferrer, Vázquez Montalbán, and Carnero. Of course, points of contact do exist between him and other poets near in age, especially Gimferrer, who has also found inspiration in Nature, especially in *Apariciones,* and who at times has cultivated the traditional hendecasyllabic line. Certainly the formal aspects of poetry have concerned all of these poets: in the sixties, they thought it their role to make formal concerns a priority in Spanish poetry. Nonetheless, Colinas will remain detached from the nucleus of his generation, at least that nucleus which Castellet's *Nueve novísimos poetas españoles* created in the minds of many readers, and, like Leopardi's poet, he may continue along a solitary path, his sights fixed on Night and Nature.

# POEMS

# ◆ GIACOMO CASANOVA ACEPTA EL CARGO DE BIBLIOTECARIO QUE LE OFRECE, EN BOHEMIA, EL CONDE DE WALDSTEIN

Escuchadme, Señor, tengo los miembros tristes.
Con la Revolución Francesa van muriendo
mis escasos amigos. Miradme, he recorrido
los países del mundo, las cárceles del mundo,
los lechos, los jardines, los mares, los conventos,
y he visto que no aceptan mi buena voluntad.
Fui abad entre los muros de Roma y era hermoso
ser soldado en las noches ardientes de Corfú.
A veces he sonado un poco el violín
y vos sabéis, Señor, cómo trema Venecia
con la música y arden las islas y las cúpulas.
Escuchadme, Señor, de Madrid a Moscú
he viajado en vano, me persiguen los lobos
del Santo Oficio, llevo un huracán de lenguas
detrás de mi persona, de lenguas venenosas.
Y yo sólo deseo salvar mi claridad,
sonreír a la luz de cada nuevo día,
mostrar mi firme horror a todo lo que muere.
Señor, aquí me quedo en vuestra biblioteca,
traduzco a Homero, escribo de mis días de entonces,
sueño con los serrallos azules de Estambul.

# ◆ GIACOMO CASANOVA ACCEPTS THE POSITION OF LIBRARIAN OFFERED TO HIM, IN BOHEMIA, BY THE COUNT OF WALDSTEIN

Please hear me, my lord, my limbs are weary.
While the French Revolution drags on, the few friends
I've got are dying. Look at me, I've traveled
the countries of the world, the prisons of the world,
the beds, the gardens, the oceans, the nunneries
and I've learned they don't accept my good intentions.
I was an abbot within the walls of Rome and it was splendid
to be a soldier in the fiery nights at Corfu.
At times I've played the violin a bit
and you know, my lord, how Venice trembles
with music and the islands and the cupolas flame.
Please hear me, my lord; from Madrid to Moscow
I've traveled in vain, the wolves of the Holy Office
are after me, a hurricane of tongues
rises behind me, venomous tongues.
And all I want is to keep a clear mind,
to smile with the light of each new day,
to show uncompromising horror at everything that dies.
My lord, I'll stay here in your library,
I'll translate Homer, write about my days back then
and dream of the blue seraglios of Istanbul.

*Sepulcher in Tarquinia* (1975)

## ◆ NOVALIS

Oh Noche, cuánto tiempo sin verte tan copiosa
en astros y en luciérnagas, tan ebria de perfumes.
Después de muchos años te conozco en tus fuegos
azules, en tus bosques de castaños y pinos.
Te conozco en la furia de los perros que ladran
y en las húmedas fresas que brotan de lo oscuro.
Te sospecho repleta de cascadas y parras.

Cuánto tiempo he callado, cuánto tiempo he perdido,
cuánto tiempo he soñado mirando con los ojos
arrasados de lágrimas, como ahora, tu hermosura.
Noche mía, no cruces en vano este planeta.

Deteneos esferas y que arrecie la música.
Noche, Noche dulcísima, pues que aún he de volver
al mundo de los hombres, deja caer un astro,
clava un arpón ardiente entre mis ojos tristes
o déjame reinar en ti como una luna.

## ◆ NOVALIS

Oh night, I haven't seen you in so long, so filled
with stars and fireflies, so drunk with perfumes.
After long years, I've come to know you in your blue
fires, in your woods of chestnut and pine.
I know you in the fury of the barking dogs
and in the damp strawberries sprouting in the dark.
I sense you filled with waterfalls and vines.

How long I've kept quiet, how much time I've lost,
how much time dreamt away, looking with eyes
filled to the brim with tears, as now, upon your beauty.
Dear Night, don't cross this planet in vain.

Pause, you spheres, and let the music swell.
Night, most sweet Night, since even now I must go back
to the world of men, let a star fall,
nail a burning harpoon between my grieving eyes
or let me reign within you like a moon.

*Translated by John DuVal*


*Sepulcher in Tarquinia* (1975)

# ◆ NOVIEMBRE EN INGLATERRA

*Happy is England . . .*
*Yet do I sometimes feel a languishment*
*For skies Italian.*

JOHN KEATS

yo sé que ahora es noviembre allá en Inglaterra,
son azules las noches y copiosas en astros,
cosa extraña pues ya la nieve va cayendo
en los montes de Escocia, voraz consume el fuego
las ramas del espino, cuelan desnudas ramas
el sol que filtran tristes las cortinas y deja
su oro viejo en los libros de vuestras bibliotecas,
aún se puede apreciar, en el fondo del prado
con escarcha, las luces de los invernaderos,
es ésta la estación más pura, ni la música,
ni el arte, ni los besos, la corrompen, sólo hay
como una expectativa inmensa sin los pájaros,
un silencio de lunas y de soles muy fríos
que sin embargo dicen al corazón que sueña
otras tierras: escúchate, aquí termina el mundo,
sublime apoteosis del respeto y las rosas,
no bajes hacia el mar que, tenebroso y húmedo,
alberga toda muerte

# ◆ *NOVEMBER IN ENGLAND*

*Happy is England*
*Yet do I sometimes feel a languishment*
*For skies Italian.*

JOHN KEATS


I know that now it is November there in England,
the nights are blue and copious in stars,
strange since the snow is already falling
in the mountains of Scotland, voracious, the fire consumes
the branches of the hawthorn, bare branches sift
the sunlight, which the sad curtains filter, and it leaves
its ancient gold in the books of your libraries,
you can still see, at the end of the meadow
with frost, the lights of the green houses,
this is the purest season, neither music,
nor art, nor kisses corrupt it, there's only
something like an immense expectation without birds,
a silence of moons and of very cold suns
which nonetheless say to the heart that dreams
other lands: listen, the world ends here,
sublime apotheosis of respect and roses,
don't go down to the sea that, dark and damp,
harbors all death


*Sepulcher in Tarquinia* (1975)

# ◆ LA CORONA

En aquellas bárbaras alturas de *La Corona*
la pureza del aire
nos recordaba el acto de respirar.

La luz desvanecía los cuerpos desgastados
y venía el olor de la nieve nocturna,
el aroma de los tizones de las cabañas incendiadas.
Se renovaba el mundo
en los ojos pasivos y negadores del rebaño de cabras
petrificado en el tiempo de la cerca,
en la maraña roja del robledal
sacudido por la ventisca y los aullidos.

(Esperábamos un atardecer
turbado por el seco resonar de las hachas
y los silbidos de las hoces en las mieses enfermas.
La noche sería aún más perfecta
en el hondo desfiladero de roca amenazada,
mientras con el carro del leñador descenderían,
con un río de sombra,
los troncos humedecidos de astros y de hielos.)

¡Qué angustia recordar el trigo muerto
entre los campanarios de pizarra,
el lago de las truchas circundado de hogueras
y, más allá, entre los álamos blancos,
las voces primitivas
de los que ahondaban en los surcos!
Atrás quedó la salmodia de las aguas conocidas,
la regularidad que ignora lo fatal.

## ◆ *LA CORONA*

In those barbarous heights of *La Corona*
the purity of the air
made us conscious of the act of breathing.

Weakened bodies faded in the light
and the smell of the night snow blew in
with the aroma of coals from the lighted cottages.
The world was renewing itself
in the passive, unreflecting eyes of the goat flock,
turned to stone in the time of the fold,
in the red tangle of the oak grove
shaken by the winds and the howls of the blizzard.

(We expected an evening
stirred by the dry echo of axes
and the whistle of scythes in the sickly wheat.
The night would be even more perfect
in the deep defile of threatened rock,
while on the woodcutter's wagon,
on a river of shadow,
the tree trunks, wet with stars and frost, would be coming
    down.)

What grief it is to remember the dead wheat
around the slate bell towers,
the trout lake circled by bonfires
and further off, among the white poplars,
the primitive voices
of those who were digging in the furrows!
Behind us lay the psalm books of known waters,
the regularity that is blind to fate.

Aquí tocas la médula del mundo
en la soledad de las piedras astilladas
y no sabes, o no quieres, leer
en una geografía de símbolos borrosos.
Es el miedo a la muerte quien detiene tus pasos
en este mediodía cruzado por soles desmesurados.
El recuerdo te azuza y te hace soñar
bella la ingrata vida de que huyes.
Observas la rotación de las águilas en las cimas
corroído de dudas, como siempre,
y, con espanto, te niegas
a sepultar tus días en el vacío de los límites.

Here you touch the marrow of the world
in the loneliness of splintered stones
and you don't know how to, or you don't want to, read
in a landscape of clouded symbols.
It is the fear of death that holds back your steps
in this midday crossed by immoderate suns.
Memory arouses you and makes you imagine
beautiful the wretched life you flee.
You watch the circling of eagles above the peaks
and as always are corroded by doubts.
Terrified, you refuse
to bury your days in the emptiness of limits.

*Translated by John DuVal*


*Astrolabe* (1979)

## ◆ EL RÍO DE SOMBRA

Este camino bordeado de abrumadoras higueras centenarias,
¿a dónde me conduce en esta noche incierta?
El calor derrotó a las palomas sobre el trigal
y sólo alza la noche su gigantesco vuelo
sobre las frescas, innumerables, cascadas de las parras,
sobre el ojo sin esperanza de la perdiz enredada
y herida en una trampa del claro del bosque,
sobre el sudor dc los caballos.
La sombra crea un río dulcísimo de sombra,
un hondo curso entre los troncos negros
que trazó una mano de inspiración divina.

Una espada enorme me persigue
en cada anochecida, desgarra el cielo, silba
endemoniada entre las ramas.
Pero hoy estoy seguro; adiós, agotadoras
insistentes insidias de la vida.
Seguro estoy en el curso insondable
del camino nocturno, entre las infinitas
líneas que alguien trazó hace ya siglos.
Un curso en el que sólo me confunde
el enfermizo, sublime aroma
de una procesión de rosales segados.

# ◆ THE RIVER OF SHADOW

This road lined with dour hundred-year-old fig trees—
where is it taking me on this uncertain night?
The heat has overcome the doves in the wheat field.
Only the night begins its gigantic flight
over the cool, innumerable cascades of grapevines,
over the unhoping eye of the partridge tangled
and wounded in a snare at the clearing,
over the sweat of the horses.
The shade creates a sweet, fresh river of shadow,
a deep channel between black trunks,
traced by a divine hand.

When night falls an enormous sword
comes after me; it tears at the sky, whistles
demonically among the branches.
But today I am safe. Goodbye, persistent
and exhausting snares of life.
Safe in the unfathomed channel
of the night road, between the infinite
lines that someone drafted centuries ago.
A channel where nothing bewilders me
but the sickly, sublime aroma
of a procession of mown rose bushes.

*Translated by John DuVal*

*Astrolabe* (1979)

# ◆ CABEZA DE LA DIOSA ENTRE MIS MANOS

*654 a. C.*

Barro oscuro conforma tu figura
que mantiene el tiempo detenido.
Ser hombre o ser dios hoy es lo mismo:
sólo un poco de tierra humedecida
a la que un sol antiguo dio dureza,
hermosura mortal, luz muy madura.
Pero lo que ha durado esta cabeza
frágil que ha contemplado tantos siglos
la muerte de los otros, que en mis manos
descansa, se hace fugazmente eterno.
En su rostro moreno cae la noche,
cae mucha luz de ocaso en sus dos labios
y cae un día más de nuestra vida.
Misterio superior este de ver
cómo su cuerpo acumula siglos
mientras el nuestro pierde juventud.
Misterio de dos barros que han brotado
de un mismo pozo y bajo un mismo fuego.
Mas sólo a uno de ellos concedió
el Arte la virtud de ser divino
y, en consecuencia, no morir jamás.

# ◆ HEAD OF THE GODDESS IN MY HANDS

*654 B.C.*

Dark clay shapes your form
that holds time still.
To be man or god, today it's all the same:
only a little damp earth
to which an ancient sun gave firmness,
mortal beauty and mellowed light.
But the time borne by this fragile head,
looking out for centuries
on the death of others, and now resting in my hands,
becomes fleetingly eternal.
Night settles on the dark face,
light from the sunset falls on her lips
and one more day of our lives falls.
A higher kind of mystery, seeing
her body gather centuries
while ours loses youth.
The mystery of two clays sprung
from the same well, from beneath the same fire.
But to only one has Art
given the virtue of being divine
and, thus, of never dying at all.

*Astrolabe* (1979)

# NOCHE MÁS ALLÁ DE LA NOCHE

## IV

Allá, entre los cipreses, sobre el lomo del mar,
veíamos saltar los felices delfines:
divinidad fulgiendo sobre un agua de plata.
Se había quedado quieto el tiempo en la orilla
de aquella mañana melodiosa del mundo.
Descendía del cielo un dulcísimo fuego
que envolvía los montes y que hacía brillar
eternas las miradas, los cuerpos fatigados.
Saltaban los delfines sobre el mar y eran signos
de los dioses sus cuerpos que la hablaban al alma.
Venía un aroma de algas en las rocas,
presencia de lo negro, esencia de la hondura.
Suavisimamente crepitaba el pinar
tras nosotros, pasaba al oído su música
de vibraciones leves, de apagados murmullos.
El aire penetraba hasta la misma médula
de los huesos y hacía arder muy lentamente
en el centro del pecho una hoguera de música.
Y, como los delfines, saltaban de la mente
nuestros mejores sueños del amor de otros días
en países lejanos, brasas de las cenizas.
Saltaban los delfines, pero nos fuimos sin
desvelar el mensaje de sus cuerpos de luz.
Leíamos la luz y, al leerla, gozábamos
de suma perfección, sin que se revelase
el secreto inmortal, divino, de la hora.
Seguimos el camino por los montes en llamas.
Los delfines saltaban encima de la muerte.

## Canto IV

Through the cypress trees, over there, we used to watch
the happy dolphins jumping over the back of the sea:
divinity flaming up on a water of silver.
And time had quietly come to rest on the shore
of that melodious morning of the world.
The tenderest fire came down from the sky, wrapped
the hills in flames, and though our bodies were tired,
caused our gaze to shine with eternal light.
The dolphins went on jumping in the sea and their bodies
became a sign of the gods that spoke to the soul.
A smell of algae was coming up from the rocks,
presence of blackness, essence of the deepest part.
The pines in the grove crackled very softly
behind us, we could hear the sound they made,
a music of slight vibrations, of muted whispers.
The air penetrated to the very marrow of our bones
and in the center of our chests a bonfire of music
was beginning to burn slowly, ever so slowly.
And the best of our dreams of love from other days
in distant countries, live coals from the ashes,
came rising up in our minds, like the dolphins on the sea.
The dolphins kept jumping up, but we walked away
without unveiling the message of their bodies of light.
We read the light and, as we read it, the highest
perfection was ours, without the immortal secret
revealing itself, divine secret of time.
We went on along the road through the hills in flames.
The dolphins went on jumping, rising over death.

ANTONIO COLINAS   211

# VIII

*Ni el amor de Penélope me saciará la sed*
*de aventura y misterio. Sabed que no he nacido*
*para vida animal.* Y por eso forzó
en sí el conocimiento, quiso verse en el rostro
sin rostro de los dioses que albergaban las aguas.
Después de haber probado las raíces del mal
en la isla de Circe, quiso ir más allá
del confín, hasta el fondo de la tumba del sol.
Y vio las costas últimas, y las últimas islas
surcando cual delfines el horizonte en llamas.
Al fin, tras las columnas de Hércules, el mar
era ya un mar sin gentes, soledad infinita.
Pero cuerpos y almas aún estaban beodos
de aventura en la proa de aquella frágil nave.
Y otra noche cayó del lado de la aurora
como un fúnebre velo, como un gran trueno negro.
Y soplaban los astros primeros en la vela
como un húmedo beso azulado de luz.
Y la luna embrujó cinco noches seguidas
sus ojos que, por fin, vieron la cima inmensa
alzada frente a ellos, la orilla de lo oscuro,
la presencia inhumana, informe, de la nada
o del todo, el nido del terror más sublime.
Y quisieron leer en aquella visión,
extraer el secreto más hondo de la cima,
mas un viento feroz se fue alzando de ella.
Un viento que excavaba una fosa en la mar.
La mar que hirvió furiosa encima de sus huesos.

## Canto VIII

*Not even the love of Penelope will quench my thirst*
*for adventure and mystery. And know that I was not born*
*for animal life.* And so it was, he forced
himself towards knowledge and tried to see himself
in the factionless face of the gods that dwell in waters.
And after having tasted the roots of evil
in the isle of Circe, he tried to go beyond
the outer limits, to the depths of the tomb of the sun.
And he saw the farthest coasts, and the farthest islands
like dolphins, circling around the burning horizon.
Beyond the Columns of Hercules at last,
the sea was a tribeless sea, endless loneliness.
But down in the bow of that fragile ship their bodies
and souls were swooning still from the draught of adventure.
Another night fell down from the side of dawn
like a funeral veil, like big, black thunder.
And like a moistened kiss of bluish light,
the first of the stars of night filled the sail.
And for five succeeding nights the moon bewitched
their eyes, till, at last, they saw the enormous peak
rise up before them, the shore of darkness,
the formless, inhuman presence of the void or perhaps
all being, the nest of the most sublime terror.
And they tried to gather something from that vision,
to extract the secret from the deepest part of the summit,
but then a furious wind rushed out from under.
A wind that began to dig a grave in the sea.
The sea that boiled up fiercely over their bones.

# IX

Confirmación de que algo divino hay en nosotros
fue el verte y comprobar que no eras el osario
de la Historia o una lección de arquitectura,
sino la geometría del alma, un soberbio
torbellino de mármol en el centro del mundo.
Por ti renunció el hombre a vagar por el ponto
y abandonó las islas de Calipso y sus ninfas,
dirigiendo las naves a tu faro de nieve,
arrastró a la locura a su mente, que luego
vagaba extraviada entre los sacros pórticos
de Epidauro, locura sombreada por laureles.
De ti brota armonía, que genera la música.
En ti nacen los números, que explican los símbolos.
Fue como ir ascendiendo de un mar de culpa y miedo
hasta el sol que abrasaba el dolor de mi noche.
Y allá arriba ardía en luz de oro el mundo,
los siglos que han sido y aquellos que serán.
Yo cerraba los ojos en busca de lo negro
que siempre hubo en mí, pero yo era lo blanco
recibido de ti, hoguera entre tus piedras.
Y perdía la noción de cuanto había sido.
Y perdí el sentido asomado a la sima
del límite, asido a un conocimiento
que, como tú, quemaba, astro caído, sed
del tiempo en la hora inmortal de mi hora.
Cerraba y abría mis ojos comprendiendo
la cristalización de los dioses: el templo,
la ruina de la luz, la tumba de la luz.

## Canto IX

Confirmation that something divine resides within us
came with seeing you and knowing for sure,
that you were not History's ossuary or a class
in architecture, but the geometry of the soul,
a proud whirlwind of marble in the center of the world.
For you, man renounced roving the sea,
left behind the islands of Calypso and her nymphs,
and turned the ships instead towards your beacon of snow,
caught up madness and dragged it into his mind,
that then wandered lost through the sacred halls
of Epidaurus, a madness shaded by laurel trees.
The harmony that inspires music flows from you.
In you, numbers are born, that explain the symbols.
It was like rising from a sea of guilt and fear
to the sun that set the pain of my night on fire.
Above the world in a light of gold, the centuries
flamed—those that have been and those to come.
Closing my eyes, I began to search for the blackness
I'd always found inside me, but I was whiteness
received from you, a bonfire rising from your stones.
And I lost the notion of all that had ever been.
And I fainted away peering over the abyss
at the edge, holding fast to what I knew
that burned the same as you, fallen star,
the thirst for time in the immortal hour of my hour.
Closing and opening my eyes, I understood
the crystallization of the gods: the temple,
the ruins of light, the tomb of light.

## XI

El cielo es aún azul, mas ya humea el Vesubio
tras los mínimos huertos sembrados de jilgueros.
Tiene la tierra fiebre de ese espeso sol rubio
que enardece las sangres y filtran limoneros.
Está firme aún él mármol y, seguros, los besos
en los besos se sacian de bocas prodigiosas.
Larga vida al amor, a los cuerpos ilesos
que, esperando la Noche, van libando las rosas.
Despacio, muy despacio, la luz última arde
en el agua que tiembla en el estanque umbroso.
Luego un gran silencio va abatiendo la tarde,
va arrastrando los cuerpos hacia el mar tenebroso.
Tiembla también la vela en los ojos del sabio
que acaba un manuscrito, y en su copa el vino
luctuoso reposa y espera su labio
el poso del veneno que lo hará ser divino.
De unos huyen las navas, de otros restan hundidas
las manos en el oro fugaz con vano empeño.
Se van quienes aún forjan ilusiones perdidas;
se quedan los beodos por la pasión y el sueño.
Al fin, se pone el cielo todo negro y se inflama,
bola de pus, el sol como el ojo quemado
por un tizón del cíclope, que furioso derrama
por su boca ceniza sobre el campo arrasado.
Del Imperio en ruinas han hecho sepultura
bajo el manto de azufre y de lava ardiente
dos cuerpos juveniles, la carne húmeda, dura,
que aún se besa, se abraza, se penetra doliente.

## Canto XI

Smoke from Vesuvius rises towards the sky, still
blue, beyond the smaller fields, sown by linnets.
The thick, white sun, though filtered by lemon trees,
makes the land feverish and kindles the blood.
The marble is still in place; the kisses, secure, quench
their thirst with kisses from splendid mouths.
A long life for love, for bodies, unbruised,
that wait for Night, drinking the juice of roses.
The last ray of light burns slowly, very slowly,
on the water trembling in the pool, in shadows.
Then, a great silence brings the evening down, and
drags away the bodies towards the tenebrous sea.
A candle also trembles in the eyes of the sage,
ending his manuscript; the mournful wine rests
in his cup; the last poisonous dregs, reaching his lips,
will make him divine. Some have hoisted their sails,
sped away; others sink their hands into fleeting gold,
in vain. Those who still forge their dreams, though lost,
have gone. Others, drunk with passion or sleep, remain.
In the end, the whole sky blackens and flames up,
the sun, a ball of pus—like the seething eye—
singed by a hot coal from the angry Cyclops,
spewing ashes from his mouth onto the leveled stalks.
In the ruins of the Empire, two youthful bodies
have made their tomb, beneath a stratum of sulphur
and burning lava, damp skin, hardened, still kisses
the other, embracing, penetrating sadly.

# XIII

Aún recuerda muy bien que cuando apareció
por vez primera ya no pudo olvidarla.
Transcurrieron después de ello muchos días
viendo cómo su espíritu natural se alteraba.
Y oyó que iban diciendo de él: *Ved cómo aquella
ha ido destruyendo la persona de éste.*
Viajó algún tiempo y luego, a su regreso,
se puso a buscarla, pero le fue negada
la ventura de verla y volvió el dolor.
Siguióse divulgando entre toda la gente
su historia y sus versos, hasta que cierto día
acaeció que estando pensativo en su casa,
después de que sus ojos mucho hubieran llorado,
ella apareció ante él y se acercó
con compasivo y pálido rostro, como de amor.
Contra aquella visión poderosa pidió
ayuda a la razón. Ambos vagaron luego
durante algún tiempo por un hermoso valle
donde hubo infinita serenidad, dulzuras.
Pero, al mismo tiempo, había en sus almas
una lucha terrible y como dolorosa.
Más tarde sucedieron y vió algunas cosas
que pronto le llevaron a no pensar en ella.
Sólo puedo deciros que había puesto sus pies
en ese espacio extremo de esta vida nuestra
más allá del que nadie puede arriesgarse a ir
si previamente quiere seguir siendo humano,
si previamente tiene intención de volver.

## Canto XIII

He remembers well, even now, that when she first
appeared, he knew that he wouldn't forget her.
And after that, many days came and went
and he could see how his natural spirit was changing.
And he heard the things the people said: *Don't you see
she's begun to destroy the very character of the man.*
He traveled for a time and, after returning home,
he began to seek her out, but it wasn't his luck
to find her, and the pain he'd felt before came again.
The story continued to spread among all the people
and his verses were heard, till on a certain day
it so happened that when he was sitting at home, deep
in thought, when many tears were shed from his eyes,
she appeared before him and came near to sit beside him
with a compassionate, pallid face, as if from love.
He then appealed to reason and tried his best
to resist the powerful image. The two of them
wandered then for a time through a beautiful valley
and there they found infinite peace and pleasantries.
But, at the same time, their souls were wrought
with something like a terrible and painful struggle.
But later on some things occurred and he saw
some things that led him to put her out of his mind.
I can only tell you that he had put his feet
in that space that lies at the very edge of our lives
which no one can take the risk of going beyond,
if beforehand he wants to keep on being human,
if beforehand he's set his mind on coming back.

# XVIII

Madrugada: caverna de la piedra musgosa
cuando en acantilados se despeña la noche
y regresa a los prados la luz sucia de lluvia,
y los hombres, durmiendo, ensayan su morir.
Siglos hace que llueve sobre la mansa yerba,
sobre la piedra viva que atenaza a otras almas
templadas con el bronce de la campana pura.
Y ver en lo sagrado lo sagrado: en el templo
la música. El templo y su retablo ardiendo
como una gigantesca y barroca custodia
con mil velas, retablo de oro y de fuego.
Y la música es la de voces no humanas
que separan la aurora de la noche, o acaso
llevan la luz al mismo corazón de la Sombra.
Va ardiendo el alba-noche de las místicas almas
como una hoguera de oro que las voces avivan.
Misterio sacro expuesto en el ojo que ve
fundida la materia, y el sueño, y el perfume
del incienso, intangible sensación que no besa.
Llueve fuera en las losas y aquí dentro el crisol
de las almas decanta arcano sacrificio
en el vapor de sangre que humedece el retablo.
Y el oro se acrecienta con la sangre que corre,
con las voces que queman y que escuecen, son llagas
en el oro de música, sol de voces que fulgen,
o que manan, o sangran de la carne maldita
del mundo, de la carne condenada y maldita
de los seres que sienten al dios, mas no lo tocan.

## Canto XVIII

Break of day: cavern of moss-covered stone
when night is thrown headlong from rocky cliffs
and the light soiled with rain goes back to the fields
and men, falling asleep, rehearse their own deaths.
The rain has fallen for years on the gentle grass,
on the living stone that clutches other souls
brought in tune with the bronze of the purest bell.
And to see the sacred part of the sacred: in the temple
the music. The temple and its radiant altarpiece
glistening like a gigantic, baroque shrine
with a thousand candles, altar of gold and fire.
And the music comes from voices that are not human,
that divide the dawn from night, or perhaps
carry the light to the very heart of the Shadow.
The dawn-night of the mystic souls begins to burn
like a blazing, golden fire that the voices stoke.
Sacred mystery disclosed in the eye that sees
the melting substance, the sleep, and the pungent smell
of incense, intangible sensation that fails to kiss.
It's raining outside on the stones and here inside
the crucible of the souls draws off the arcane sacrifice
in steam from the blood that dampens the altarpiece.
And the gold begins to grow with the blood running
with the burning, stinging voices; these are wounds
in the gold of the music, sun of voices burning,
or springing forth, or bleeding from the cursed flesh
of the world, from the condemned and cursed flesh
of beings that sense the god, but do not touch.

## XX

Aquí, en Arabí, el agua de la fuente
del Olvido me turba la memoria y la sangre.
Y tumbado a la sombra sin sombra del olivo
pierdo el conocimiento y, al perderlo, lo adquiero.
Oh, sí, yo estuve ya en esta ebullición
de pájaros, en la hora escabrosa del monte.
O quizás, algún día, gozando estaré
sin fin de este fuego en este mismo espacio.
Sensación de sentirse inmortal, si no fuera
que, a veces, de los labios se escapan, en la paz
de este paraíso sublime, unos versos:
*Mientras brille la sangre bajo el sol, esa sangre*
*el sol la incendiará, la beberá la tierra.*
Pero aún se detiene el tiempo y yo soy tiempo.
Y sonámbulo entrego mi vida a lo sonámbulo.
Y veo el pozo blanco que sabe del secreto
de mi vida deshecha en vidas ensoñadas;
el pozo que contiene el misterio, pues él,
arrastrando a lo arcano, sacia la sed del alma.
Al alba mis pestañas tiemblan con el oscuro
zureo de las palomas. Y sé que a mediodía
el dulzor del azahar y el susurro del agua
no me dejan pensar. Y sé que a la tarde
la siesta puede ser tan larga, tan profunda,
que cuando me despierte rechazaré la vida
y ansiaré más sueño de sueño enloquecido.
Y sé que a la noche, como los ruiseñores,
no lograré dormirme en la sombra estrellada.

## Canto XX

Here in Araby, the water of the fountain
of Oblivion disquiets my memory and my blood.
And lying in the shadeless shadow of the olive tree
I lose consciousness, and lost, I find it.
Yes, I've been here before at the time when the birds
come bursting forth, at the rugged hour of the forest.
Or perhaps, some day, I'll find myself taking
eternal pleasure from this fire in this same space.
Sensation of thinking oneself immortal, except
that now and then, in the peace of the sublime paradise,
some lines of verse seem to escape from my lips:
*While the blood glistens beneath the sun, the sun*
*will set the blood on fire and the earth will drink it.*
But time still comes to a halt and I am time.
A somnambulist, I hand over my life to somnambulism.
And I see the white well that has known the secret
of my life, broken apart into lives that I've dreamed;
the well that contains the mystery, yes, that one,
dragging the secret out, quenches the thirst of the soul.
The lashes of my eyes tremble at dawn with the dark
cooing of the doves. And at midday, I'm sure the sweet
smell of the orange flowers and the murmur of the water
will not let me think. And in the afternoon,
my sleep can be so long and so profound,
that when I wake up, I put off living
and long to sleep some more with sleep gone mad.
And I know at night, like the nightingales, I won't
be able to fall asleep in the starlit shade.

*Night Beyond Night* (1982)

# NOTES

## Introduction

1. "Hay 'nuevos' poetas españoles que a unas influencias y educaciones poéticas determinadas, unen sus experiencias nuevas, su posición moral nueva, condicionada por una perspectiva histórica distinta, por ejemplo, a la generación crítica de los años cincuenta." For the convenience of the English-speaking audience, translated quotations have been cited in the text. The original Spanish version of short quotations is contained parenthetically in the text; longer quotations are contained in notes.

2. "Quizá mi generación vuelva los ojos nuevamente a temas y procedimientos que preocupaciones éticas más urgentes hicieron desoír a algunos en un pasado no muy lejano."

3. "Entre nosotros aún andan mezcladas demasiadas cosas, tan mezcladas que dudo ya que nunca quede claro algún aspecto, por pequeño que sea, de nuestra cultura nacional."

4. "Un fantasma recorre la poesía española. Para unos el fantasma es un libro: *Nueve novísimos*. Para otros, el fantasma es el cerco de desprecio o de ira que ese mismo libro solivianta en muchos de sus abundantes lectores."

5. ". . . el reflejo de un incipiente neocapitalismo ya arraigado en Cataluña."

6. In the last few years, the *novísimos*, as a group and as individual poets, have received a great deal of critical attention. *Insula* dedicated its January 1989 issue to the *novísimos*, with articles by Víctor García de la Concha, Andrew P. Debicki, José Olivio Jiménez, and other important critics.

7. In *Nueve novísimos* (51), Castellet used the following unidenti-

fied translation: "'Soy uno de tantos entre los miles de jóvenes de mi clase . . . en cuyo cerebro fermentan ciertas ideas. Nada en mí tiene el menor viso de originalidad. Soy muy joven y muy ignorante; no hace más que escasos meses que empecé a especular sobre la posibilidad de una revolución con hombres que seguramente han reflexionado sobre el conjunto de la situación mucho más que yo. Soy una mera partícula en la gris inmensidad de las gentes. Sólo tengo la buena fe que me anima y el vigoroso deseo de ver consolidarse la justicia', concluyó Jacinto."

## Pere Gimferrer

1. Gimferrer confirmed this information, summarized from his "Poética" in *Nueve novísimos poetas españoles*, during my interview with him in May, 1985.

2. Since 1970, Gimferrer has written poetry in Catalan and then translated it to Castilian. *Poesía 1970–1977* is a bilingual edition that includes *Els miralls, Hora foscant, Foc cec, Tres poemes* and *L'espai desert. Aparicions/Apariciones y otros poemas* was published bilingually in 1982. His last volume, *El vendaval* (1988), translated to Castilian by other poets, including Octavio Paz, Antonio Colinas, and Jaime Siles, is to be published by Ediciones Península in 1989.

3. "Hay una anécdota famosa en la que intervinieron Mallarmé y un pintor o un músico, no recuerdo, Delacroix o Ravel. El que fuese le dijo al poeta que le gustaría mucho escribir pero que le faltaban las ideas, a lo que Mallarmé contestó que la poesía no se hacía con ideas sino con palabras. También Roland Barthes afirmó que el escritor no es el que tiene algo que decir sino el que tiene algo que escribir."

4. "Este poema es / una sucesión de celadas: para el / lector y para el / corrector de pruebas / y para / el editor de poesía. / Es decir, / que ni a mí me han dicho lo / que hay detrás de las celadas, porque / sería como decirme el dibujo / del tapiz, y esto / ya nos ha enseñado James que no / es posible." The title of the Catalan original is "Paranys," first published in *Els miralls*. The numbers in parentheses refer to pages rather than lines.

## Manuel Vázquez Montalbán

1. This quotation from my interview with Vázquez Montalbán in October of 1976 was stated as follows: "cuaja el mito del amor que cada día hay que renovar."

2. "... quisiera que cantaras la muerte de Macorina sobre un colchón tripudo / las hojas de maíz / salientes por los descosidos del mundo."

3. "... fruta para labios agostados / para manos / sin otro mundo que llevarse al alma."

4. "... no escogí nacer entre vosotros / en la ciudad de vuestros terrores."

## Guillermo Carnero

1. I have used the second edition of Carnero's collected poetry, *Ensayo de una teoría de la visión,* for all poems cited in the text.

2. "... pero yo sé que nada hay de ti entre tus libros, / en tus palabras, nada puede saberse, nada / puedes mostrar."

3. "... decidme si merecía la pena haber vivido para esto, / para seguir girando en el suave chirrido de las tablas alquitranadas, / para seguir girando hasta la muerte."

4. "Producir un discurso / ya no es signo de vida, es la prueba mejor / de su terminación. / En el vacío / no se engendra discurso, / pero sí en la conciencia del vacío."

5. This epigraph to the poet's first volume, *Dibujo de la muerte,* is taken from Guy du Faur de Pibrac.

## Antonio Colinas

1. My impressions of Colinas's views on poetry are based primarily on my interview with the poet in Madrid in May, 1985.

2. "... la madera, la carne, el agua y las piedras, / tal como son: materia y signo del Gran Todo. / Signo de algo total que nunca te han nombrado, / signo real (no un sueño, pues soñar aún no sabes), / imágenes hermosas en un espejo roto / que nadie, hasta ahora, ha logrado reunir / con armonía tal que apacigüe al humano." Unless otherwise indicated, poems are quoted from Colinas's collected poetry, *Poesías, 1967–1981.*

3. "Hoy pienso que la poesía es algo así como el puro y llano testimonio de sentimientos expresados sobre la tierra y entre las piedras, es decir, en el espacio en que nos ha tocado vivir reducido a su mayor elementalidad."

To avoid confusion, I should point out that Colinas's use of "testimonio," a word so often employed by the "social" poets, does not refer in this case to political or social statement but rather to the poet's semi-oracular power to speak from, to, and about the cosmos. Nonetheless, his use of the term seems ambiguously provocative: it could possibly be a remonstrance to the *novísimos*, who rejected the concept of poetry as testimony, or to the "social" poets, who limited the scope of their testimony to the social dimension of man.

4. Colinas's original words, taken from the interview referred to in note 1, were "ese espacio sin fechas, sin nombres en el que hacemos las grandes preguntas, en el que lanzamos los grandes gritos."

5. "Rilke nos dejó dicho que la poesía es *un proceso de purificación y de crecimiento,* una *realidad misteriosa* cuya existencia perdura al lado de la nuestra que desaparece."

# WORKS CITED

Batlló, José. *Antología de la nueva poesía española*. Madrid: El Bardo, 1968.

———. *Antología de la nueva poesía española*. 3rd ed. Barcelona: Lumen, 1977.

———. *Poetas españoles poscontemporáneos*. Barcelona: El Bardo, 1974.

Bousoño, Carlos. Prologue. *Ensayo de una teoría de la visión*. By Guillermo Carnero. 2nd ed. Madrid: Hiperión, 1983. 11–68.

Carnero, Guillermo. *Dibujo de la muerte*. 2nd ed. Barcelona: Ocnos, 1971.

———. *El Azar Objetivo*. Madrid: Visor, 1974.

———. *El Sueño de Escipión*. Madrid: Visor, 1971.

———. *Ensayo de una teoría de la visión*. 2nd ed. Madrid: Hiperión, 1983.

———. *Variaciones y figuras sobre un tema de La Bruyère*. Madrid: Visor, 1974.

Castellet, José María. *Nueve novísimos poetas españoles*. Barcelona: Barral, 1970.

———. *Veinte años de poesía española 1939–1959*. Barcelona: Seix Barral, 1960.

Colinas, Antonio. *Astrolabio*. Madrid: Visor, 1979.

———. *Leopardi*. Madrid: Júcar, 1974.

———. *Noche más allá de la noche*. Madrid: Visor, 1982.

———. *Poemas de la tierra y de la sangre*. León: Diputación Provincial, 1969.

———. *Preludios a una noche total*. Madrid: Adonais, 1969.

———. *Poesías, 1967–1981*. 2nd ed. Madrid: Visor, 1984.

————. *Sepulcro en Tarquinia*. León: Provincia, 1975.

————. *Truenos y flautas en un templo*. San Sebastián: Caja de Guipúzcoa, 1972.

Delgado, Agustín, et al. *Equipo "Claraboya": Teoría y poemas*. Barcelona: El Bardo, 1970.

Eliot, T. S. "*Ulysses*, Order, and Myth." *Critiques and Essays on Modern Fiction 1920–1951*. Ed. John W. Aldridge. New York: Ronald Press Co., 1952. 426–27.

García Martín, José Luis. *Las voces y los ecos*. Madrid: Júcar, 1980.

G[arcía] Moral, Concepción, and Rosa María Pereda. *Joven poesía española: Antología*. Madrid: Cátedra, 1979.

Gimferrer, Pere. *Apariciones y otros poemas. Edición bilingüe*. Madrid: Visor, 1982.

————. *Arde el mar*. Barcelona: El Bardo, 1966.

————. *La muerte en Beverly Hills*. Barcelona: El Bardo, 1968.

————. *Poemas 1963–1969*. Barcelona: Ocnos, 1969.

————. *Poesía 1970–1977 (edición bilingüe)*. Madrid: Visor, 1978.

————. "Poética." *Nueve novísimos poetas españoles*. Ed. José María Castellet. Barcelona: Barral, 1970. 155–58.

Grande, Félix. *Apuntes sobre poesía española de posguerra*. Madrid: Taurus, 1970.

González Muela, Joaquín. *La nueva poesía española*. Madrid: Alcalá, 1973.

Guerrero Martín, José. "Borrador: Pere Gimferrer: 'El mundo no sería el mismo sin Rimbaud.'" *Diario de Avisos* [Canary Islands] 8 Aug. 1985: 14.

James, Henry. *The Princess Casamassima*. London: Macmillan and Co., 1886.

Jiménez, José Olivio. *Diez años de poesía española (1960–1970)*. Madrid: Insula, 1972.

————. Prologue. *Poesías, 1967–1981*. By Antonio Colinas. 2nd ed. Madrid: Visor, 1984. 9–49.

Jongh Rossel, Elena de. *Florilegium: Poesía última española*. Madrid: Austral, 1982.

Martín Pardo, Enrique. *Antología de la joven poesía española*. Madrid: Pájaro Cascabel, 1967.

————. *Nueva poesía española*. Madrid: Scorpio, 1970.

Martínez García, Francisco. *Historia de la literatura leonesa*. Madrid: Everest, S. A., 1982. 1084–1113.

Martínez Ruiz, Florencio. *La nueva poesía española: antología crítica: segunda generación de postguerra, 1955–1970*. Madrid: Biblioteca Nueva, 1971.

Millán, Fernando, and Jesús García Sánchez. *La escritura en libertad.* Madrid: Alianza, 1975.

Pozanco, Víctor. *Nueve poetas del resurgimiento.* Barcelona: Ambito, 1976.

———. *Segunda antología del resurgimiento.* Barcelona: Ambito Literario, 1980.

Prieto, Antonio. *Espejo del amor y de la muerte: antología de poesía española última.* Madrid: Azur, 1971.

Romero, Amelia. *Doce jóvenes poetas españoles.* Barcelona: El Bardo, 1967.

Rubio, Fanny, and José Luis Falcó. *Poesía española contemporánea: Historia y antología 1939–1980.* Madrid: Alhambra, 1981.

Solner, G. L. *Poesía española hoy.* Madrid: Visor, 1982.

Urbano, Manuel. *Antología consultada de la nueva poesía andaluza (1963–1978).* Sevilla: Aldebarán, 1980.

Vázquez Montalbán, Manuel. *A la sombra de las muchachas sin flor* Barcelona: El Bardo, 1973.

———. *Coplas a la muerte de mi tía Daniela.* Barcelona: El Bardo, 1973.

———. *Movimientos sin éxito.* Barcelona: El Bardo, 1969.

———. *Praga.* Barcelona: Ocnos, 1982.

———. *Una educación sentimental.* 2nd ed. Barcelona: El Bardo, 1969.

Warren, Robert Penn. *Band of Angels.* New York: Random House, 1955.